Patterns of Suicide and Homicide in America

Patterns of Suicide and Homicide in America

by
David Lester

Nova Science Publishers, Inc.

Art Director: Christopher Concannon
Graphics: Elenor Kallberg and Maria Ester Hawrys
Book Production: Michael Lyons, Roseann Pena,
Casey Pfalzer, June Martino,
Tammy Sauter, and Michelle Lalo
Circulation: Irene Kwartiroff, Annette Hellinger,
and Benjamin Fung

Library of Congress Cataloging-in-Publication Data

Lester, David, 1942-
Patterns of suicide and homicide in America / David Lester.
p. cm.
Includes bibliographical references (p.) and index.
ISBN 1-56072-148-0 : $59.00
1. Suicide--United States--Regional disparities.
2. Homicide--United States--Regional disparities.
3. Suicide. 4. Homicide.
I. Title.
HV6548.U5L453 1993 93–20946
362.2'82'0973--dc20 CIP

6080 Jericho Turnpike, Suite 207
Commack, New York 11725
Tele. 516-499-3103 Fax 516-499-3146
E Mail Novasci1@aol.com

Printed in the United States of America

Patterns of Suicide and Homicide in America

David Lester

CONTENTS

Chapter 1

INTRODUCTION

The sociological study of suicide rates is based in part upon the assumption that different societies have very different suicide rates and that these suicide rates remain stable over time. If these conditions are met, then societal suicide rates are amenable to study.

The particular societies chosen vary. Ideally, of course, societies consist of different nations or primitive societies. Thus, Stack (1980e) studied the influences of urbanization, economic development, and the proportion of the elderly on the suicide rates of nations by means of a multiple regression analysis. He found that only economic development and the age structure were significantly related to the national suicide rates.

Palmer (1971) explored correlates of suicide rates in primitive non-literate societies, reporting that suicide rates were associated with other measures of aggression such as homicides, assaults and dueling. Suicide rates were not related to child-rearing practices.

The success of this type of study led investigators to explore correlates of the suicide rates of smaller regions within a country. Studies have been conducted of states (Breault, 1986) and counties in the USA (Pescosolido and Mendelsohn, 1986), for example, and on wards or census tracts within one city (Newman, et al., 1973).

Such studies may be seen as simply extending to smaller regions a methodology developed on nations. However, investigators often talk of different regions within a culture as having unique subcultures, thereby applying the theoretical notions that guided the cross-national studies to these smaller regions.

There may be some truth to the notion of subcultures, since regions within nations do differ considerably in social characteristics. Furthermore, the division of a country into regions may be no less artificial than the way in which some nations have been created in the course of history, so that even today, some nations seem torn apart by internal strife between the regions, while others feel kinship with neighboring regions in other countries.

THE PRESENT BOOK

The Sample: States

The present book presents an examination of the variation in the suicide rate of the continental states of the USA. It uses the theory of suicide proposed by Durkheim (1897) to explain societal suicide rates and follows him in applying it to regions within a nation.

The continental states are chosen, excluding Alaska and Hawaii, since it is easier to migrate (and even commute) between the continental states, and since the inclusion of the two new states introduces two states with very different social characteristics into the sample.

Spatial Autocorrelation

It has recently been pointed out by Odland (1988) that the states are not independent in the way that forty eight unrelated subjects are, and so the techniques of correlational analysis may no longer be valid. Certainly the states are not spatially independent with respect to the social variables studied here [see, for example, Lester (1989b) for a study of the spatial autocorrelation of state suicide rates]. However, the present set of analyses do include the longitude and latitude of each state (as measured by the longitude and latitude of each state capital) as two variables, thereby exploring simple linear spatial associations.

Suicide and Homicide

The present set of analyses focuses on both suicide and homicide rates. This is done for three reasons. First it provides an examination of two important violent behaviors, each worthy of study. Second, the examination of two behaviors permits the specificity of the results to be explored. Are the correlates of suicide rates the same as or different from those of homicide rates?

Third, Lester (1987b) has explored the theories and empirical work suggesting that suicide and homicide may be behaviors generated by similar etiological factors differing only in the direction in which the aggression is directed (Henry and Short, 1954).

Incidentally, the suicide and homicide rates of the states do remain quite stable over time. The Pearson correlations between the rates in 1970 and in 1980 are 0.85 for suicide and 0.88 for homicide, and so one of the preconditions for studying the social correlates of these rates is met.

Factor-Analysis

The present book rejects the techniques of regression analysis (the favorite tool of both economists and sociologists these days) for factor analysis. The reason for this is that regression analysis is better suited to predicting a dependent variable rather than understanding its causation.

For example, multiple regression selects variables which are the most powerful correlates of the dependent variable and then explores whether other variables add any significant predictive power. Let us take four variables later used in this book (alcohol consumption, church attendance, divorce rates, and interstate migration rates), and explore how a multiple regression analysis deals with them. A total regression of all four variables on the state suicide rates leads to the following result:

	beta	t	significance
alcohol consumption	-0.012	0.13	0.9000
church attendance	-0.103	1.09	0.2800
divorce rates	0.393	3.19	0.0030
interstate migration	0.467	3.71	0.0006

The multiple regression analysis indicates that only divorce and inter-state migration play a significant role in predicting suicide rates. However, we will see in Chapter 2 that all four variables are intercorrelated and form a cluster (or factor) that correlates as a whole with suicide rates. The simple Pearson correlation coefficients demonstrate this quite clearly:

	alcohol consumption	church attendance	divorce rates	interstate migration
alcohol consumption	-	-0.37*	0.40*	0.50*
church attendance	-	-	-.049*	-0.43*
divorce rates	-	-	-	0.74*
suicide rate	0.42*	-0.49*	0.78*	0.80*

* statistically significant at the 5% level or better

It can be seen that all four social variables correlate with the state suicide rates, and with one another. Such an analysis suggests that there may be some underlying social characteristic, such as Durkheim's notion of social integration, that causes this association between indices of social integration and suicide rates. Such a conclusion is not possible with multiple regression analyses.

Of course, correlational analyses of whatever type cannot prove cause and effect. (Only experimental studies in which the investigator manipulates the values of the independent variables can do that.) However, correlational analyses can support theoretical propositions.

Plan of The Book

In the first section of this book, a set of social variables will be used to characterize the states of the USA, and a factor analysis will identify seven factors (or clusters) of these variables, factors which are orthogonal (independent), that is, the seven factor scores have zero correlation with one another.

Then these factor scores will be correlated with suicide and homicide rates, overall and for various subgroups of the population (men and women, whites and blacks, and the young and old). In addition, several other theoretical possibilities will be examined, such as the differences in the social correlates of suicide by different methods (for example, firearms versus hanging).

In Part Two, the generality of the findings identified in Part One will be explored in three separate international comparisons: England, Hungary and Sri Lanka. The question asked is whether the factor-analytic patterns identified for the USA are found also in other countries.

In Part Three, the generality of the findings is extended to other types of data sets: time series data of the USA, variation over counties within a state and variations over nations. In Part Four, the methodology is applied to other social problems such as alcohol consumption and the death penalty.

Finally, in Part Five, the most important theoretical implications of the present studies are explored. It is argued that the present book provides strong support for Durkheim's theory of suicide, stronger than other methodologies have previously supplied.

Part One: The Basic Studies

Chapter 2

THE REGIONAL VARIATION OF SUICIDE AND HOMICIDE

Suicide and homicide rates show a wide variation over the states of America. The states, therefore, provide a convenient sample of regions to use for an ecological study of suicide and homicide (or, to use alternative terms, a societal, regional or aggregate cross-sectional study). In addition, social data for these states are relatively easy to obtain from published sources. The present book describes a series of regional studies of suicide and homicide rates in the USA, and the present chapter reports the primary study.

Durkheim's (1897) theory of suicide in societies was based on two dimensions. Suicide was hypothesized to be common in societies in which the degree of social integration (that is, the strength of the individual's social network) was very low (egoistic suicide) or very high (altruistic suicide). Similarly, suicide was hypothesized to be very common where the degree of social regulation (that is, the degree to which the individual's attitudes and values are shaped by the society) was very low (anomic suicide) or very high (fatalistic suicide).

Durkheim's theory has been used to predict a variety of associations between suicide rates and social indicators. For example, societies with large numbers of migrants appear likely to have lower degrees of social integration than societies with more stable populations. Similarly, societies with high rates of divorce appear likely to have lower degrees of social integration, and so higher suicide rates. Stack (1980a, 1980b) has confirmed that states in the USA with higher rates of interstate migration and higher rates of divorce do indeed have higher rates of suicide.

Religion appears to reflect both social regulation and social integration, although it is unclear whether particular denominations involve more social regulation and social integration than others. Stack (1980c) found no relation between the proportion of Roman Catholics in the states of the USA and suicide rates. Lester (1987c), however, looked at measures of *religiosity* (for example, church attendance) and found a strong association between church attendance and suicide rates in the states.

Lester has replicated many of Stack's studies, adding homicide rates to the analyses. Lester (1987a) found, for example, that religious denomination was associated with homicide rates over the states of the USA whereas suicide rates were not. In addition, homicide rates have strong correlates with social indicators such as the degree to which the states have a southern subculture (Lester, 1986-1987).

In all of the studies conducted by Stack and Lester, a large number of variables have been included in the correlation analyses which select the most powerful *predictors* of suicide rates. A factor analysis, on the other hand, groups all of the variables having strong intercorrelations together and permits an examination of how many clusters of social indicators exist and the extent to which they correlate with the target variables, in this case rates of personal violence.

Accordingly, as discussed in Chapter 1, the present study was undertaken to explore how the social indicators used by Stack, Lester, and others in their earlier studies relate to rates of personal violence (suicide and homicide) using factor analysis.

Method

Suicide and homicide rates for 1980 for each of the continental states of the USA were obtained from the National Center for Health Statistics (1985) and supplemented in the other studies reported in this book by direct analysis of the data tapes of all death certificates in the USA in 1980 provided by the National Center for Health Statistics. The suicide and homicide rates for the states of America in 1980 are shown in Table 2.1.

Table 2.1 Suicide and homicide rates in 1980.

	suicide	homicide		suicide	homicide
AL	11.2	15.9	MI	11.5	10.9
AZ	16.9	10.5	MN	10.8	02.9
AR	11.6	11.2	MS	09.9	14.3
CA	14.5	14.6	MO	11.9	12.4
CO	16.3	06.8	MT	14.5	05.3
CT	08.9	05.5	NE	10.1	04.3
DE	11.9	07.9	NV	22.9	16.7
FL	15.4	15.5	NH	11.0	01.8
GA	12.6	14.8	NJ	07.4	07.2
ID	13.1	03.5	NM	17.4	16.1
IL	09.3	12.5	NY	09.5	12.6
IN	10.4	08.1	NC	11.2	11.4
IA	11.0	02.7	ND	11.0	02.0
KS	10.9	07.7	OH	11.9	07.6
KY	12.8	09.2	OK	13.1	11.1
LA	12.1	16.5	OR	14.6	05.4
ME	12.5	03.2	PA	11.1	07.0
MD	10.8	10.1	RI	11.2	05.9
MA	08.2	04.5	SC	09.5	12.4

	suicide	homicide		suicide	homicide
SD	12.7	03.5	VA	13.4	09.2
TN	12.2	12.0	WA	13.3	05.5
TX	12.3	17.1	WV	12.5	08.2
UT	13.2	04.0	WI	11.7	03.1
VT	14.7	03.3	WY	16.0	06.4

The independent variables are those used by Stack, Lester and other investigators in previous studies, supplemented by other social and economic variables that appeared to be of potential interest. They were obtained for 1980 primarily from the *Statistical Abstract of the United States* which is published annually by the US Government Printing Office.

The 1984 *Statistical Abstract* provided the data for divorce rates (Table 122), interstate migration from 1975 to 1980 (Table 16), the percent black (Table 37), the birth rate (Table 87), the percentage vote for the Republican candidate for President, Reagan (Table 418), the percent urban population (Table 25), the median family income (Table 770), the death rate and infant mortality rates (Table 106), and the population density (Table 12); the 1982-1983 *Statistical Abstract* provided the per capita income (Table 705) and the crime rate (Table 289); the 1981 *Statistical Abstract* provided the unemployment rates, overall and for males and females (Table 638), the percent over 65 years of age (Table 31), participation in the labor force by males, females and overall (the employment ratio) (Table 638), and the population (Table 9); the 1988 *Statistical Abstract* provided the personal income per capita.

The percent of people separated/divorced, the percent under 15 years of age, the percent born in-state, the percent born abroad, the ratio of females to males, the median age, and the percent in poverty were obtained from the *Census of the United States*, 1980 conducted by the Census Bureau and published by the US Government Printing Office

The strictness of state handgun control laws were taken from Lester (1987c), church attendance and the percent Roman Catholics from Quinn, et al. (1982), the latitude and longitude of each state capital from Lester (1980a), the index of southernness from Gastil (1971), the gross state product per capita from Renshaw, et al. (1988), and the alcohol consumption per capita from (Anon, 1985).

Results

The Pearson product-moment correlations are shown in Table 2.2. It can be seen that suicide rates were strongly correlated with divorce rates, interstate migration, the percentage born in state, and the ratio of females to males, and less strongly with twelve other variables.

Table 2.2 Correlations between social indicators and rates of personal violence

social indicator	suicide rate	homicide rate
divorce rate	0.78*	0.40*
interstate migration	0.80*	0.02
median family income	-0.08	-0.20
% black	-0.30*	0.68*
church attendance	-0.49*	-0.26*
% Roman Catholic	-0.10	-0.23
birth rate	0.34*	-0.01
% vote for Reagan	0.35*	-0.18
southernness	0.20	0.77*
% urban population	0.08	0.29*
% separated	-0.15	0.55*
% divorced	0.81*	0.32*
per capita income	-0.01	-0.11
% over 65 years	-0.33*	-0.18
females in labor force	0.08	-0.38*
males in labor force	0.14	-0.42*
gun control laws	-0.57*	-0.07
population	-0.19	0.42*
population density	-0.50*	-0.08
latitude	-0.09	-0.80*
longitude	0.60*	0.06
alcohol consumption	0.42*	-0.07
death rate	-0.45*	-0.01
% under 15 years	0.14	0.02
% born in state	-0.68*	-0.09
% foreign born	0.01	0.16
infant mortality	-0.37*	0.56*
median age	-0.19	0.02
% in poverty	-0.02	0.51*
gross state product	0.34*	0.07
personal income	0.04	-0.09
unemployment rate	-0.11	0.23
male unemployment	-0.10	0.14
female unemployment	-0.12	0.33*
employment ratio	0.16	-0.40*
crime rate	0.42*	0.35*
females/males	-0.64*	0.19

* significant at the 5% level or better

Homicide rates were strongly correlated with the percentage of blacks in each state, latitude and southernness, and less strongly with thirteen other variables.

The social variables were factor-analyzed using SPSSX with a principal components extraction and a varimax rotation to identify independent (orthogonal) factors. Seven factors were identified with eigen values greater than one (see Table 2.3). The factor scores for each factor were correlated with the homicide and suicide rates, and the results are shown in Table 2.4.

Naming factors is somewhat arbitrary. However, Factor I appears to measure urbanization and personal wealth, Factor II lack of social integration, Factor III age structure, Factor IV southernness, Factor V participation in the labor force, Factor VI unemployment, and Factor VII Roman Catholicism.

Table 2.3 Results of the factor analysis (with decimal points omitted)

	Factor						
	I	II	III	IV	V	VI	VII
median family income	74#	-04	-01	-14	58#	08	-11
% urban	92#	09	-08	13	-01	-05	06
per capita income	79#	08	21	-14	48#	-07	-16
population	62#	-19	14	25	-16	18	-40
population density	54#	-38	37	11	08	07	44#
personal income	80#	14	23	-13	47#	-07	-13
% in poverty	-50#	-06	-13	47#	-54#	02	01
gross state product	42#	26	-28	-09	33	-29	-33
% immigrants	86#	08	23	-03	-10	01	18
% Roman Catholic	60#	-08	32	-32	16	06	45#
% born in state	-40#	-81#	05	07	-12	19	-12
crime rate	72#	53#	-01	17	05	05	15
divorce rate	-02	88#	-16	02	-03	-01	-08
interstate migration	-04	83#	-27	-10	11	-32	13
church attendance	-10	-73#	-20	-20	-19	-33	21
% divorced	15	91#	-08	-07	06	13	-16
gun control strictness	27	-58#	18	13	13	20	-08
alcohol consumption	31	53#	14	-16	39	-15	35
females/males	10	-50#	55#	34	-31	21	26
longitude	10	50#	-54#	-28	-07	-09	-38
birth rate	-14	11	-92#	-14	-12	-18	-10
% voting for Reagan	05	23	-58#	-33	-08	-45#	-05
% over 65 years	-05	-22	69#	-29	-51#	-20	-02
death rate	-10	-32	79#	-05	-43#	-01	-04
% under 15 years	-32	-05	-91#	-01	-12	06	02
median age	31	03	92#	-02	-15	-01	01
southern index	-26	27	-12	73#	-30	11	-34
% separated	26	-04	18	84#	12	14	15
% black	-10	-16	04	92#	-10	13	-01
latitude	02	-13	08	-77#	43#	16	05
infant mortality rate	05	-25	17	82#	-17	15	01
females in labor force	12	10	-02	-15	81#	-32	14
males in labor force	19	03	-34	-26	80#	-29	-01
employment ratio	03	08	-15	-20	75#	-47#	02
unemployment rate	01	-05	03	07	-20	96#	-01
male unemployment	07	-07	06	-07	-17	93#	-08
female unemployment	-06	-01	-03	27	-21	88#	12
% of variance	26%	21%	13%	8%	7%	5%	3%

high loading (greater than 0.40)

The correlations between the factor scores and suicide and homicide rates are shown in Table 2.4. Homicides rates were significantly correlated with factors scores for Factors II and IV and V, positively with social disintegration and southernness and negatively with labor force participation. In contrast, suicide rates were significantly correlated only with Factor II, positively with social disintegration.

Table 2.4 Correlations between factor scores and suicide and homicide rates

		suicide	homicide
Factor I	urban/wealth	-0.02	0.18
Factor II	social disintegration	0.85*	0.29*
Factor III	age	-0.24	-0.07
Factor IV	southern	-0.11	0.73*
Factor V	labor force participation	-0.03	-0.37*
Factor VI	unemployment	-0.07	0.10
Factor VII	Roman Catholic	-0.04	-0.17

* significant at the 5% level of better

Discussion

This study has shown that many variables correlate with rates of personal violence. Suicide rates were associated most strongly with the amount of interstate migration and the percent divorced. Homicide rates were most strongly associated with latitude and the percentage of black residents in each state. However, it is difficult to obtain a sense of the *general* social correlates of suicide and homicide rates from an examination of the list of significant correlates shown in Table 2.2.

In contrast, the factor analysis showed that a number of variables were loaded meaningfully of several of the major clusters. Suicide was associated with a factor which had divorce rates and interstate migration as the variables with the highest loadings. It seems inappropriate to select one of these variables as the most critical for suicide, since states with high divorce rates also had the highest rates of interstate migration (Pearson r = 0.74) and both correlated strongly with the suicide rate (r = 0.78 for the divorce rate and 0.80 for interstate migration, correlations which are not significantly different from each other).

It is clear that the correlates of homicide and suicide are very different from one another. This study gives little support for the hypothesis that suicide and homicide are opposed behaviors having parallel but opposite correlations with critical socio-economic variables as has been suggested (Lester, 1987b). (The suicide and homicide rates were only weakly associated, r = 0.24.)

A more useful way of conceptualizing the pattern of correlations between rates of personal violence and socioeconomic variables is to see the states of the USA as having different cultural patterns. To pick out one of the components of a pattern as supporting a particular hypothesis from theory and as the most important variable in predicting rates of personal violence obscures the fact that these components are related and are part of a broader cultural pattern.

It is supportive of Durkheim's theory of suicide that one factor was identified (Factor II) which appeared to measure social integration. Interestingly, no factor was identified which appeared to measure social regulation. However, the factors extracted depend to a large extent on the variables chosen for the analysis. Perhaps no variables pertinent to social regulation were contained in the present data set, although it is difficult to locate social variables characteristic of the states which might measure social regulation. We will see later that variables relevant to social regulation are available for selection for a cross-national study modelled on the present state study (see Chapter 16).

Chapter 3

SUICIDE AND HOMICIDE RATES OF MEN AND WOMEN

The suicide rates of women vary greatly across America. For example, as can be seen in Table 3.1, both male and female suicide rates were highest in Nevada in 1980 and lowest in New Jersey. The ratio of the male suicide rate to the female suicide rate ranged from 1.95 in Nevada to 5.95 in South Dakota.

Homicide rates also vary considerably in the states of America, as can be seen in Table 3.1, with the male/female homicide rate ratio ranging from 1.06 in Maine to 6.04 in West Virginia.

In this chapter I will explore which social and economic variables are associated with the female suicide and homicide rates and the male-to-female rate ratios.

Correlates Of The Female Suicide And Homicide Rates

In Chapter 2, it was shown that a variety of social variables are associated with the suicide and homicide rates of the states of America. In some regional studies, primarily of the census tracts in single cities, the male and female suicide rates have been found to have different correlates. For example, Diggory and Lester (1976) studied census tracts in Buffalo and reported that the male suicide rate was associated with the incidence of the widowed and divorced and the incidence of unemployed males. The female suicide rate, in contrast, was associated with the median family income.

For the present study, the social and economic variables used in Chapter 2 were explored for their association with male and female suicide rates. The product-moment correlations of these variables with the male and female suicide rates over the continental states in 1980 are shown in Table 3.2.

It can be seen that both male and female suicide rates were associated with similar variables: the divorce rate, interstate migration, church attendance, the percent voting for Reagan as President, the incidence of divorced people, the percent of elderly, longitude, the death rate, the percent born in state, the gross state product per capita, the female/male ratio, population density, alcohol consumption, and the strictness of state handgun control laws.

Table 3.1 Suicide and homicide rates for males and females for the USA in 1980

	suicide rate		male/female	homicide rate		male/female
	male	female	ratio	male	female	ratio
AL	19.3	3.7	5.22	25.1	7.5	3.35
AZ	26.3	7.8	3.37	15.7	5.5	2.85
AR	18.5	5.2	3.56	16.7	6.0	2.70
CA	21.4	7.7	2.78	24.0	5.5	4.39
CO	25.2	7.4	3.41	9.8	3.8	2.56
CT	14.2	4.0	3.55	9.0	2.2	4.04
DE	17.8	6.5	2.74	11.5	4.5	2.54
FL	23.0	8.4	2.74	25.6	6.3	4.07
GA	19.9	5.8	3.43	23.8	6.4	3.72
ID	21.7	4.7	4.62	4.5	2.1	2.31
IL	15.1	3.9	3.87	21.1	4.4	4.76
IN	17.5	3.8	4.61	13.4	3.1	4.35
IA	19.0	3.5	5.43	3.8	1.6	2.38
KS	16.6	5.5	3.02	12.4	3.1	4.07
KY	20.7	5.3	3.91	14.9	3.7	4.00
LA	19.8	5.0	3.96	27.2	6.5	4.18
ME	20.3	5.2	3.90	3.3	3.1	1.06
MD	17.0	4.9	3.47	17.0	3.6	4.76
MA	12.9	4.0	3.22	7.3	2.0	3.70
MI	18.0	5.3	3.40	16.7	5.5	3.05
MN	17.0	4.9	3.47	3.8	2.1	1.80
MS	14.9	3.8	3.92	23.1	6.1	3.77
MO	19.0	5.3	3.58	20.0	5.4	3.69
MT	23.2	5.8	4.00	8.4	2.3	3.68
NE	17.0	3.5	4.86	5.7	2.9	2.01
NV	30.1	15.4	1.95	22.2	11.1	2.00
NH	17.4	4.9	3.55	3.1	0.6	4.95
NJ	12.7	2.5	5.08	11.7	3.0	3.93
NM	28.5	6.7	4.25	27.6	5.0	5.52
NY	14.4	5.1	2.82	22.0	4.2	5.23
NC	17.4	5.3	3.28	18.4	4.8	3.83
ND	18.0	4.0	4.50	2.7	1.2	2.23
OH	18.7	5.6	3.34	12.1	3.5	3.41
OK	19.9	6.5	3.06	17.6	4.9	3.59
OR	23.7	5.8	4.09	7.1	3.8	1.86
PA	18.1	4.7	3.85	11.4	3.0	3.86
RI	17.1	5.8	2.95	8.2	3.8	2.14
SC	15.2	4.2	3.62	20.4	4.9	4.19
SD	22.0	3.7	5.95	5.9	1.1	5.15
TN	19.0	5.9	3.22	19.8	4.6	4.32
TX	19.3	5.5	3.51	28.1	6.4	4.38
UT	19.3	7.2	2.68	5.5	1.4	2.26
VT	23.3	6.5	3.58	5.6	1.1	4.93
VA	21.6	5.5	3.93	13.7	4.9	2.78
WA	20.5	6.2	3.31	7.8	3.3	2.35
WV	20.6	4.8	4.29	14.4	2.4	6.04
WI	18.6	5.1	3.65	4.2	2.1	2.00
WY	24.1	7.4	3.26	8.7	3.9	2.22

Table 3.2 Correlates of the male and female suicide and homicide rates in 1980

	suicide rate		male/female suicide rate	homicide rate		male/female homicide rate
	male	female		male	female	
divorce rate	0.69*	0.80*	-0.32*	0.31*	0.62*	-0.14
interstate migration	0.74*	0.71*	-0.28*	-0.05	0.25*	-0.28*
median family income	-0.17	0.10	-0.25*	-0.21	-0.13	-0.14
% black	-0.34*	-0.16	-0.07	0.69*	0.57*	0.26*
church attendance	-0.45*	-0.48*	0.30*	-0.23	-0.36*	-0.04
% Roman Catholic	-0.13	0.01	-0.13	-0.21	-0.25*	0.07
birth rate	0.36*	0.18	0.06	-0.03	0.02	-0.19
% voting for Reagan	0.33*	0.27*	0.05	-0.21	-0.08	-0.22
southernness	0.21	0.16	-0.10	0.76*	0.67*	0.30*
% urban population	-0.04	0.32*	-0.45*	0.27*	0.32*	-0.09
% separated	-0.24	0.04	-0.28*	0.56*	0.47*	0.28*
% divorced	0.71*	0.82*	-0.42*	0.23	0.54*	-0.20
per capita income	-0.12	0.19	-0.31*	-0.12	-0.03	-0.12
% elderly	-0.28*	-0.30*	0.20	-0.14	-0.23	0.05
labor force:						
females	0.01	0.18	-0.15	-0.42*	-0.19	-0.35*
males	0.10	0.15	-0.02	-0.45*	-0.29*	-0.26*
handgun control strictness	-0.58*	-0.44*	0.12	-0.03	-0.16	0.14
population	-0.24*	-0.03	-0.23	0.46*	0.23	0.32*
population density	-0.56*	-0.26*	-0.08	-0.05	-0.13	0.12
latitude	-0.07	-0.13	0.13	-0.81*	-0.67*	-0.33*
longitude	0.60*	0.44*	-0.03	0.01	0.19	-0.30*
alcohol consumption	0.31*	0.52*	-0.33*	-0.12	0.08	-0.08
death rate	-0.42*	-0.37*	0.20	0.04	-0.09	0.24
% under 15 years	0.19	-0.04	0.17	0.01	-0.01	-0.09
% born in state	-0.60*	-0.70*	0.39*	-0.03	-0.26*	0.16
% foreign born	-0.10	0.22	-0.38*	0.17	0.10	0.14
infant mortality	-0.40*	-0.23	-0.07	0.59*	0.41*	0.32*
median age	-0.23	-0.02	-0.11	0.04	0.02	0.14
% in poverty	0.05	-0.15	0.18	0.53*	0.34*	0.34*
gross state product	0.28*	0.34*	-0.20	0.04	0.13	-0.14
personal income	-0.07	0.24	-0.32*	-0.11	-0.02	-0.09
unemployment	-0.09	-0.11	0.05	0.23	0.20	0.10
male unemployment	-0.07	-0.10	0.05	0.15	0.11	0.10
female unemployment	-0.09	-0.12	0.06	0.32*	0.31*	0.07
employment ratio	0.11	0.18	-0.07	-0.43*	-0.26*	-0.28*
crime rate	0.29*	0.60*	-0.56*	0.31*	0.46*	-0.11
females/males	-0.63*	-0.46*	0.02	0.24*	0.01	0.35*

* significant at $p < 0.05$ or better

The female suicide rate was also associated with the percent of the population that was urban. The male suicide rate was also associated with the percent black, the birth rate, the population of the state, and infant mortality. It can be seen, therefore, that the similarities in the correlates of male and female suicide rates outweigh the differences.

The correlates of male and female homicide rates are also shown in Table 3.2. Male homicide rates were most strongly associated with the percentage of blacks, southernness, and latitude, as were female homicide rates. Female homicide rates appeared to be more strongly associated with the indices of social disintegration (interstate migration, church attendance, and the percentage of divorced people, for example) than male homicide rates.

The Male/Female Rate Ratios

The correlations of the male/female suicide rates with the social and economic variables are shown in Table 3.2. The male/female suicide rate ratio was positively associated with church attendance and the percentage born in state and negatively associated with the divorce rate, interstate migration, urbanization, the percentage of people separated and divorced, the crime rate, the median family income, the per capita income, the percentage foreign born and alcohol consumption.

The male/female homicide rate ratio was not strongly associated with any variable, the largest coefficient being 0.35 with the female/male population ratio and with female participation in the labor force.

Associations With The Social Factors

The correlations between the seven factor scores identified in Chapter 2 and the male and female suicide and homicide rates are shown in Table 3.3.

Table 3.3 Correlations of the factor scores with the male and female suicide and homicide rates

suicide rate			**suicide rate**	
		male	**female**	**m/f ratio**
Factor I	urban/wealth	-0.12	0.20	-0.37*
Factor II	social disintegration	0.78*	0.81*	-0.36*
Factor III	age	-0.25*	-0.12	-0.03
Factor IV	southern	-0.17	0.02	-0.21
Factor V	labor force participation	-0.07	0.03	-0.07
Factor VI	unemployment	-0.04	-0.08	0.02
Factor VII	Roman Catholic	-0.07	0.03	-0.07
homicide rate			**homicide rate**	
		male	**female**	**m/f ratio**
Factor I	urban/wealth	0.18	0.15	0.03
Factor II	social disintegration	0.21	0.50*	-0.15
Factor III	age	-0.05	-0.07	0.15
Factor IV	southern	0.74*	0.62*	0.31*
Factor V	labor force participation	-0.40*	-0.23	-0.22
Factor VI	unemployment	0.10	0.11	0.04
Factor VII	Roman Catholic	-0.18	-0.12	-0.02

* significant at the 5% level or better.

It can be seen that male and female suicide rates were both correlated with Factor II (social disintegration). Male suicide rates, however, were also correlated with Factor III (age), but this correlation was much weaker than the correlation of the male suicide rate with Factor II.

The correlations of the factor scores with the male and female homicide rates of the states are also shown in Table 3.3 and can be seen to be somewhat different. Factor IV (southernness) was the strongest correlate for both sexes. In addition, Factor II (social disintegration) was associated with female homicide rates while Factor V (labor force participation) was associated with male homicide rates.

Discussion

Both male and female suicide rates varied greatly over the states of the continental USA, both increasing with the measure of social disintegration. Male suicide rates varied also with the age structure of the state populations.

Similarly, the ratio of the male suicide rate to the female suicide rate varies over the states of the USA. The male/female suicide rate ratio was higher in the less urban/wealthy states and in the states with less social integration.

The results using the male/female rate ratios were not especially interesting and did not seem to stimulate interesting hypotheses for future study.

It is difficult to speculate, even *post hoc,* about the reasons for the different patterns of correlations identified for males and females in this ecological study. Furthermore, since the empirical findings in this study are correlational, the results do not provide answers about the *causes* of the differences between male and female suicide rates. However, it is hoped that the study will stimulate hypotheses and further research on the topic.

An Investigation Of The Use Of Sex-Specific Social Variables

The first study presented in this chapter used social variables the majority of which were not sex-specific. Variables such as the divorce rate do not distinguish between men and women. This second study explored seven social variables which could be measured separately for men and women: median age, the percentage divorced, the percentage of whites, the percentage of those over 25 years of age who finished high school, the median income of those over 15 years of age with income, participation in the labor force. and the unemployment rate. Data were obtained for men and women separately from the reports of the 1980 Census (PC80-1-B and PC80-1-C).

The factor analyses (using the SPSSX Factor program with a PC extraction and a varimax rotation) for men and for women both identified three factors (see Table 3.4). However, the composition of the three factors was different for men and for women. For example, for men, the percentage of divorced men loaded on a factor along with the percentage of high school graduates, median income and participation in the labor force (Factor I). For women, the percentage of divorced women loaded on a factor along with median income only (Factor II). However, factor scores on both of these factors were associated with suicide rates.

Table 3.4 Factor analyses and correlates with rates of personal violence for sex-specific social variables

	Factor			Pearson Correlation with	
Men	I	II	III	Suicide	Homicide
median age	-0.06	0.22	0.87#	-0.12	-0.04
% divorced	0.54#	0.42	-0.01	0.71*	0.23
% white	0.38	-0.33	0.62#	0.10	-0.84*
% high school graduates	0.88#	0.18	0.19	0.30*	-0.44*
median income	0.82#	0.15	0.12	-0.08	-0.20
labor force partic.	0.76#	-0.50	-0.16	0.10	-0.45*
unemployment	-0.02	0.84#	0.04	-0.07	0.15
Correlation With:					
suicide rate	0.32*	0.14	-0.11		
homicide rate	-0.31*	0.52*	-0.43*		
Women					
median age	-0.05	0.03	0.95#	-0.11	0.03
% divorced	-0.07	0.81#	-0.18	0.78*	0.58*
% white	0.77#	-0.22	-0.04	0.01	-0.67*
% high school graduates	0.79#	0.31	-0.28	0.28*	-0.39*
median income	0.10	0.84#	0.41	0.38*	0.30*
labor force partic.	0.67#	0.44	-0.03	0.18	-0.19
unemployment	-0.76#	0.09	-0.13	-0.12	0.31*
Correlation With:					
suicide rate	0.09	0.64*	-0.18		
homicide rate	-0.60*	0.52*	-0.02		

loading higher than 0.50
* significant at the 5% level or higher

The factor scores associated with homicide rates were more different. In particular, the factors mentioned in the preceding paragraph (Factor I for men and Factor II for women) correlated in *opposite* directions with the male and female homicide rates respectively.

Looking at the associations between each of the seven sex-specific social variables and rates of personal violence, only divorce and high school graduation correlated significantly for both sexes with suicide rates, and racial composition and high school graduation with homicide rates.

This study, therefore, has suggested that examining sex-specific social variables might open up possibilities for accounting for the rates of personal violence for men and for women. Different correlates and predictors may eventually be identified for the regional variations in the rates of personal violence for men and for women which may further our understanding of the differences in the ways in which these rates are determined for the two sexes.

Chapter 4

SOCIAL CORRELATES OF LETHAL AGGRESSION

Whereas many researchers have explored the correlates of regional suicide rates or of regional homicide rates, Whitt (1969; Whitt, et al., 1972) suggested that suicide rates and homicide rates could be summed to give a measure of the lethal aggression rate of a society. Regardless of the direction in which aggression is expressed, inwardly as suicide or outwardly as homicide, some societies have high rates of lethal aggression whereas others have low rates. The direction in which the aggression is expressed is a separate variable and may have very different correlates from the lethal aggression rate. (Field [1963] proposed a similar idea.) Whitt (1985) argued that the correlates of the lethal aggression rate might well be very different from those of the component parts of the rate (the homicide rate and the suicide rate).

In his original study, Whitt hypothesized that the lethal aggression rate of a society would vary directly with the proportion of frustrated individuals in the society. The ratio of the suicide rate in the society to the lethal aggression rate should vary with the extent to which individuals in the society perceive themselves to have control over the outcomes in the society or the reinforcements that they seek. In a study of census tracts in Atlanta, the lethal aggression rate was found to vary inversely with the median family income in line with his hypothesis.

Whitt argued that industrialization was most consistent with Protestantism. Thus, in a sample of nations, Whitt predicted and found that the lethal aggression rate varied inversely with urbanization-industrialization in Protestant nations, while there was no association in Catholic nations. (There were too few nations to explore whether the association was negative in non-Christian nations.)

The present study sought to test the validity of Whitt's ideas using the continental states of America in 1980 and the data set described in Chapter 2. In addition to using Whitt's measure of the direction of aggression, the measure proposed by Field (of simply subtracting the rates) was also included in the analyses. Three measures were used: the sum of the suicide and homicide rates as a measure of the total lethal aggression, and both the difference in the rates (the suicide rate minus the homicide rate) and the ratio of the suicide rate to the lethal aggression rate as measures of the direction of aggression.

Lethal Aggression Versus Homicide

First, Table 4.1 shows the intercorrelations of the rates of aggression. It can be seen that the rate of lethal aggression correlates very highly with the homicide rate (r = 0.90) and moderately with the suicide rate (r = 0.64). The direction of aggression measures correlate more strongly with the homicide rate than the suicide rate. Thus, for the states, Whitt is incorrect in asserting that the lethal aggression rate is different from the homicide rate. The two rates are highly correlated.

Table 4.1 Pearson correlations between the measures of aggression

	homicide rate	lethal aggression rate (S+H)	direction (S-H)	direction S/(S+H)
suicide rate	0.24	0.64***	0.34**	0.15
homicide rate	-	0.90***	-0.84***	-0.90***
lethal agression rate	-	-	-0.50***	-0.64***
direction (S-H)	-	-	-	0.96***

Looking at correlates of these rates, Table 4.2 shows that the lethal aggression rate is correlated with scores on Factor II (social disintegration), Factor IV (southern) and Factor V (labor force participation) just as are the homicide rates. The direction of aggression correlates with scores on Factor IV (southern) and Factor V (labor force participation) in a direction opposite to the correlations for the homicide rate.

Table 4.2 Pearson correlations between factor scores and aggression rates

	Factor						
	I	II	III	IV	V	VI	VII
All States							
S+H	0.13	0.62*	-0.16	0.52*	-0.30*	0.05	-0.16
S-H	-0.18	0.20	-0.07	-0.77*	0.34*	-0.14	0.14
S/(S+H)	-0.22	0.02	-0.05	-0.79*	0.32*	-0.18	0.18
suicide	-0.02	0.85*	-0.24	-0.11	-0.03	-0.07	-0.04
homicide	0.18	0.29*	-0.07	0.73*	-0.37*	0.10	-0.17
Low Catholicism							
S+H	-0.39	0.09	0.61*	0.68*	0.06	-0.11	-0.34
S-H	0.62*	0.09	-0.53*	-0.80*	-0.02	-0.04	0.05
S/(S+H)	0.54*	0.08	-0.62*	-0.81*	-0.05	0.02	0.16
suicide	0.64*	0.29	-0.20	-0.61*	0.0	-0.22	-0.35
homicide	-0.55*	-0.02	0.58*	0.78*	0.04	-0.02	-0.17
High Catholicism							
S+H	0.15	0.36	-0.91*	0.50*	-0.72*	0.31	-0.49
S-H	-0.70*	0.45	0.55*	-0.85*	0.49	-0.13	0.63*
S/(S+H)	-0.72*	0.44	0.57*	-0.79*	0.55*	-0.23	0.62*
suicide	-0.44	0.83*	-0.59*	-0.15	-0.41	0.24	-0.02
homicide	0.44	0.02	-0.85*	0.74*	-0.70*	0.26	-0.62*

* one-tailed significance < 0.05 or better

Table 4.2 **Continued**

Factor Labels			
I	urban/wealth	V	labor force participation
II	social disintegration	VI	unemployment
III	age	VII	Roman Catholicism
IV	southern		

Thus, it appears that the correlates of Whitt's measures of lethal aggression and the direction of aggression are similar to those of the homicide rates, contrary to his assertion.

States High Versus Low In Catholicism

The twelve states with the lowest proportion of Roman Catholics (with a mean percentage of 7 percent) and the twelve states with the highest proportion of Roman Catholics (with a mean percentage of 67 percent) were identified, and correlations between Whitt's measures of aggression and the factor scores compared (see Table 4.2).

The critical factor for Whitt's hypothesis is Factor I (urban/wealth). The lethal aggression rate was not correlated with scores on this factor for either group of states. Thus, Whitt's hypothesis concerning the relationship between urbanization-industrialization and lethal aggression rates as a function of Roman Catholicism was not confirmed for the states of the USA.

Conclusion

Whitt's assertion that the lethal aggression rate provides an important and different variable from the simple homicide rate was not confirmed. Furthermore, Whitt's hypothesis about the relationship between urbanization-industrialization and lethal aggression rates dependent upon religion was also not confirmed. However, Whitt's suggestions are worth consideration in future research for they provide alternative conceptualizations of the variables which may, in different data sets, prove to be of interest.

Chapter 5

SOCIAL CORRELATES OF YOUTH SUICIDE AND HOMICIDE

The phenomenon of rising youth suicide rates in the USA during the 1970s and 1980s has become the major issue in suicidology. The media have given the problem a great deal of attention, and magazines and journals for those involved in mental health have all had articles on the topic. This attention is not unwarranted. The teenage suicide rate rose 287 percent from 1960 to 1980 in the USA (Maris, 1985) while the suicide rate of older Americans decreased during this same period.

Much of the research on youth suicide has replicated the research on adult suicides. Like adult suicides, youth suicides have been found to be depressed, psychiatrically disturbed and from chaotic childhoods. Occasional studies do identify features of the youth suicide that differ from the adult suicide. For example, Davis (1983) found that youth suicides are angrier at others than are adult suicides, and their suicidal actions are more impulsive and more often in response to interpersonal crises.

However, many research studies fail to find correlates of youth suicide that are found for adult suicide. For example, Lester (1988b) found that, whereas national adult suicide rates are high in nations with a higher quality of life, national youth suicide rates are not associated with the quality of life. Phillips (1984) found that the temporal variation in youth suicide was not similar to that found for adult suicides. For example, youth suicides did not show an increased incidence on Mondays or a decreased incidence on national holidays.

As a result, it is of interest to explore whether the social correlates of the regional variation of youth suicide rates in the USA are similar to those of adult suicide rates. The present study was designed to explore whether the correlates of state suicide rates reported in Chapter 2 would be found also for youth suicide.

Results And Discussion

The Pearson correlation coefficients between the factor scores for the set of social variables identified in Chapter 2 and the suicide rates by age and sex are shown in Table 5.1.

It can be seen that the suicide rates of all age groups were associated with the social disintegration factor. Where social disintegration was higher, the suicide rates of most age groups were also higher. In addition, many of the suicide rates were associated with the age factor. The younger the population in a state, the higher the suicide rate for many of the age groups, both young and old it should be noted. Furthermore, both the suicide rates of those aged 15-25 and those aged 75-85 were associated with the southern factor.

Table 5.1 The correlations of the factor scores with the suicide rates and homicide rates

	Factor						
	I	II	III	IV	V	VI	VII
Suicide Rates							
males:							
15-24	-0.05	0.57*	-0.28*	-0.32*	-0.01	-0.11	0.12
25-34	0.16	0.58*	-0.34*	-0.05	-0.27*	0.09	0.11
35-44	-0.10	0.64*	-0.19	0.01	-0.09	0.14	-0.04
45-54	-0.25*	0.52*	-0.27*	0.04	0.06	-0.04	-0.09
55-64	-0.21	0.38*	-0.28*	0.03	-0.02	-0.17	-0.21
65-74	-0.22	0.50*	-0.48*	0.01	0.03	-0.02	-0.32*
75-84	-0.15	0.53*	-0.38*	-0.24*	0.10	-0.04	-0.12
85+	-0.14	0.26*	0.13	0.01	0.09	0.20	-0.01
females:							
15-24	0.01	-0.05	-0.04	-0.17	0.16	-0.10	-0.11
25-34	0.09	0.73*	-0.01	0.16	0.14	-0.06	-0.01
35-44	0.08	0.63*	-0.09	-0.13	0.17	-0.02	0.19
45-54	0.12	0.49*	-0.40*	-0.10	-0.08	-0.14	-0.11
55-64	0.01	0.31*	-0.21	-0.13	-0.12	-0.11	0.11
65-74	0.21	0.52*	-0.24*	0.07	-0.07	0.14	-0.02
75-84	0.37*	-0.05	-0.07	0.06	-0.33*	0.01	0.14
Homicide Rates							
males:							
15-24	0.34*	0.21	-0.07	0.56*	-0.43*	0.09	-0.22
25-34	0.15	0.17	-0.05	0.72*	-0.40*	0.08	-0.16
35-44	0.05	0.08	-0.01	0.72*	-0.49*	0.12	-0.14
45-54	-0.01	0.21	-0.04	0.74*	-0.46*	0.03	-0.10
55-64	0.01	0.13	-0.04	0.84*	-0.17	0.13	-0.17
65-74	0.04	0.27	-0.12	0.62*	-0.08	0.09	-0.19
75-84	-0.19	0.19	0.07	0.23	-0.02	0.26*	0.11
85+	0.13	0.48*	0.02	0.07	-0.01	0.13	0.08
females:							
15-24	0.20	0.44*	0.10	0.50*	-0.25*	0.19	-0.07
25-34	0.16	0.50*	-0.18	0.57*	-0.26*	0.13	-0.15
35-44	-0.05	0.45*	0.06	0.61*	-0.30*	0.18	-0.10
45-54	-0.07	0.20	-0.10	0.57*	-0.38*	-0.13	-0.01
55-64	-0.07	0.06	-0.19	0.64*	-0.11	0.13	0.01
65-74	0.17	0.27*	-0.11	0.36	0.13	0.07	-0.03
75-84	0.17	0.05	0.08	0.29*	-0.25	0.21	-0.08
85+	0.27*	-0.01	-0.24	0.10	-0.09	0.07	0.14

Factor labels:

Factor I	urban/wealth	Factor II	social disintegration
Factor III	age	Factor IV	southern
Factor V	labor force participation	Factor VI	unemployment
Factor VII	Roman Catholicism		

* significant at the 5% level or better

Thus, the present study indicated that the social correlates of youth suicide rates in the USA are similar to those of adult suicide rates. It should be noted that the relative rarity of female suicide as compared to male suicide in the USA makes the state rates for female suicides unreliable when measured for a single year. This unreliability is probably responsible for the fewer significant associations identified for female suicide rates in the present study.

Homicide Rates

An analogous study was conducted for homicide rates by sex and age, and the results are shown in Table 5.1. It can be seen that scores from Factor IV (southern) correlated strongly with the homicide rates of all age groups up to 65-74 for both sexes. Similarly, scores on Factor V (labor force participation) correlated with the homicide rates of all age groups up to 45-54.

In addition, however, the analysis by age showed that, for young women, homicide rates also were associated with scores on Factor II (social disintegration).

Thus, again, the major correlate of homicide rates (Factor IV - southern) was strongly associated with the rates for almost all age groups. As with the suicides rates, the homicide rates by state for the elderly are based on very few homicides, and so the rates may be quite unreliable.

Chapter 6

SUICIDE AND HOMICIDE IN WHITES AND BLACKS

Lester (1987d) reported that suicide rates of blacks were higher in states where there was a smaller proportion of blacks. But there has not been much attention given in the USA to the differences in the correlates of state rates of suicide and homicide for whites and for blacks. The first study sought to examine the predictors of suicide and homicide rates for whites and blacks in the USA using the methodology illustrated in Chapter 2 of first factor-analyzing relevant social variables and then correlating factor scores with the rates of personal violence using the data set described in Chapter 2.

Because the population of blacks in the states can be quite small, suicide and homicide rates for blacks were calculated for a three-year period, 1979-1981. The suicide and homicide rates for whites and blacks are shown in Table 6.1.

Table 6.1 Rates of personal violence for whites and blacks (per 100,000 per year)

	Whites		Blacks			Whites		Blacks	
	Suicide	Homicide	Suicide	Homicide		Suicide	Homicide	Suicide	Homicide
AL	13.79	9.29	4.59	34.23	NE	10.53	3.09	10.33	12.40
AZ	18.74	9.86	10.67	41.01	NV	24.70	13.99	10.78	52.94
AR	12.96	7.04	5.15	31.37	NH	11.21	1.87	6.27	0.00
CA	17.56	13.17	10.35	49.66	NJ	8.18	4.42	4.35	27.32
CO	17.89	6.07	10.08	30.73	NM	21.07	18.72	7.29	38.51
CT	9.50	4.14	3.79	25.30	NY	10.70	8.41	5.54	41.08
DE	13.53	6.56	6.00	17.48	NC	12.94	7.09	5.63	24.78
FL	17.55	10.45	4.97	44.65	ND	10.39	1.12	0.00	0.00
GA	8.84	8.49	5.41	33.47	OH	12.35	4.50	9.57	35.59
ID	13.64	3.55	9.20	0.00	OK	14.05	8.97	7.21	38.60
IL	10.61	6.35	5.74	46.03	OR	15.06	5.10	6.07	33.05
IN	10.81	4.90	6.09	42.19	PA	11.60	3.48	8.26	38.81
IA	11.17	2.15	9.59	31.77	RI	11.49	5.91	10.88	16.31
KS	11.48	6.00	5.75	37.86	SC	11.55	7.59	4.19	22.03
KY	13.32	7.75	5.88	27.75	SD	10.94	0.78	0.00	0.00
LA	15.18	8.52	5.73	38.20	TN	13.51	7.77	5.85	32.23
ME	12.43	3.06	15.98	15.98	TX	14.83	14.45	5.22	47.73
MD	12.16	4.84	6.76	28.44	UT	13.67	3.69	2.71	29.81
MA	8.52	3.79	5.31	25.31	VT	14.80	3.35	22.03	22.03
MI	12.25	4.80	8.49	49.56	VA	15.23	5.60	7.29	23.15
MN	10.82	2.46	9.84	29.99	WA	13.79	4.66	12.55	32.92
MS	11.64	6.93	3.83	27.41	WV	12.70	7.41	6.53	25.75
MO	12.73	6.40	6.13	63.24	WI	11.97	2.25	5.60	25.19
MT	13.92	4.05	41.99	28.00	WY	16.13	6.05	0.00	7.43

Study One

Results

The correlations between the factor scores are shown in Table 6.2. For the total sample of 48 continental states, the suicide rates of whites and blacks were both associated with Factor II (social disintegration) in the expected direction. In addition, while white suicide rates were associated with Factor III (age), black suicide rates were associated with Factor IV (southern). Since the percentage of blacks also loaded highly on Factor IV, this latter result is congruent with Lester's (1987d) report on black suicide rates being higher in states where there were few blacks.

Table 6.2 Correlations between factor scores and black and white rates of suicide and homicide

	FACTOR						
	I	II	III	IV	V	VI	VII
Correlations: All States							
white suicide rate	0.10	0.81*	-0.25*	0.08	-0.12	-0.04	-0.04
black suicide rate	-0.10	0.26*	0.13	-0.26*	0.06	0.14	0.09
white homicide rate	0.25*	0.48*	-0.16	0.46*	-0.37*	0.02	-0.09
black homicide rate	0.41*	0.21	0.07	0.29*	-0.25*	0.29*	-0.35*
States With % Black > 9.9%							
white suicide rate	-0.11	0.61*	0.14	0.07	-0.36	-0.36	-0.29
black suicide rate	0.19	-0.07	-0.01	-0.42*	0.40*	0.46*	-0.44*
white homicide rate	0.01	0.36	-0.18	0.21	-0.48*	-0.50*	-0.24
black homicide rate	0.38	0.06	0.05	-0.59*	-0.37	0.15	-0.59*

labels:
I urban/wealthy
II social disintegration
III age
IV southern
V labor force participation
VI unemployment
VII Roman Catholicism

* statistically significantly at the 5% level or better

When only the nineteen states with black populations greater or equal to ten percent were studied, the pattern of correlations changed dramatically. While white suicide rates still correlated with scores on Factor II (social disintegration), black suicide rates now correlated with scores on Factors IV (southern), V (labor force participation), VI (unemployment) and VII (Roman Catholicism).

For the total sample of 48 continental states, white and black homicide rates were correlated with scores on Factors I (urban/wealthy), IV (southern) and V (labor force participation). White homicide rates were also associated with Factor II (social disintegration), while black homicide rates were also associated with Factors VI (unemployment) and VII (Roman Catholicism).

Reducing the sample of states to those with large black populations changed the pattern of correlations a little. White homicide rates still correlated with scores on Factor V (labor force participation), but now correlated with scores on Factor VI (unemployment) rather than IV (southern). Black homicide rates still correlated with scores on Factors IV (southern) and VII (Roman Catholicism), but no longer with scores on Factors I, V and VI.

Discussion

This study has shown that the social correlates of suicide over the states of the USA are sometimes similar and sometimes different for whites and for blacks. For example, both white and black suicide rates are associated with indices of social disintegration, but black suicide rates are associated with southernness while white suicide rates are associated with the age structure of the states.

For homicide rates, correlates of black and white homicide rates again showed some similarities, with homicide rates being higher for both groups in the south and in urban/wealthy states. However, differences also emerged, with white homicide rates varying with social disintegration while black homicide rates varied with unemployment.

This study has shown, therefore, that social correlates of white and black mortality rates from personal violence are different over the states of the USA. In particular, the standard deductions from Durkheim's (1897) theory of suicide, that suicide rates are higher where there is less social integration and regulation, appear to hold true more clearly for white suicide rates. In addition, while a southern subculture (Gastil, 1971) appears to be related to higher homicide rates in both blacks and whites, the southern subculture is associated with lower suicide rates only in blacks.

Study Two

The first study used social indicators from the states based on the total population of the state. This second study took a smaller set of variables and located measures for both whites and blacks individually. For example, while Study One examined the association between the total unemployment rate and white and black rates of personal violence, Study Two examines white unemployment rates and black unemployment rates separately.

Data Sources

Data were obtained from the publications resulting from the 1980 Census, published by the Census Bureau, for blacks and whites separately: the percentage of people over 25 years of age with four years of college completed, the male unemployment rate, the median family income, the fertility rate for women aged 35-44 ever married, the participation of women over 16 years of age in the labor force, the percentage of divorced and of separated men over 15 years of age, and the extent of inter-state migration from 1975 to 1980.

Results

The results of the factor analysis, using SPSSX with a principal components extraction and a varimax rotation, are shown in Table 6.3. For the whites, four factors were identified: I education/wealth, II social disintegration, III fertility, and IV unemployment. For the blacks, only three factors were identified: I education/wealth, II education/migration, and III unemployment/divorce. Factor I appears to be similar for both races, but the remaining factors differ considerably.

Table 6.3 Factor analysis of social variables for blacks and for whites

	Whites				Blacks		
	I	II	III	IV	I	II	III
college education	0.84#	0.07	0.13	-0.24	0.65#	0.65#	-0.06
male unemployment	-0.09	-0.01	-0.10	0.96#	-0.14	-0.57#	0.65#
med. fam. income	0.82#	-0.13	0.26	0.19	0.87#	0.09	0.31
fertility	-0.04	-0.09	-0.92#	0.08	-0.92	-0.11	0.05
females in labor force	0.77#	0.26	0.04	-0.09	0.72#	0.31	0.01
% divorced	0.06	0.91#	0.13	0.21	0.19	0.18	0.91#
% separated	0.31	-0.03	0.82#	-0.04	-0.04	-0.96#	-0.11
migration	0.10	0.90#	-0.06	-0.23	0.44#	0.83#	-0.03
Pearson r's							
suicide	0.01	0.80*	0.14	0.03	0.31*	0.20	0.15
homicide	-0.12	0.47*	0.42*	-0.07	-0.10	-0.54*	0.34*

high loading (> 0.40)
* significant at the 5% level or better

The correlations between factor scores and rates of suicide and homicide were also quite different. For example, suicide rates for whites were associated with the social disintegration factor (Factor II), whereas suicide rates for blacks were associated with education/wealth (Factor I).

Similarly, examination of the Pearson correlations between each social variable and rates of suicide and homicide revealed differences for blacks and whites (Table 6.4). Black suicide rates, but not white suicide rates, were associated with education, wealth and fertility. Black homicide rates, but not white homicide rates, were associated with education and unemployment.

Table 6.4 Pearson correlations between social variables and suicide and homicide rates

	Suicide		Homicide	
	whites	blacks	whites	blacks
college education	0.17	0.35*	0.09	-0.48*
unemployment	0.02	-0.09	-0.15	0.43*
med. fam. income	-0.05	0.32*	0.01	-0.04
fertility	-0.10	-0.38*	-0.40*	0.13
females in labor force	0.07	0.16	-0.11	-0.24
% divorced	0.76*	0.25*	0.58*	0.27*
% separated	0.20	-0.25*	0.28*	0.47*
migration	0.75*	0.26*	0.34*	-0.59*

* significant at the 5% level or better

Discussion

The social correlates of black versus whites rates of personal violence are somewhat different. The traditional associations for the total United States population described in Chapter 2 are seen to be true only for whites.

An explanation of the different patterns for blacks is probably a result of the composition of blacks in states with high rates of suicide and low rates of homicide, primarily states with small proportions of blacks (Lester, 1987d). Lester (1988d) has shown that blacks in the states where blacks are rare (such as Maine, Vermont and Montana) tend to be migrants and well-educated, and much more similar in general to the whites in those states than are the blacks in states where blacks are numerous. It would appear that different sociological theories may be needed to account for the regional differences of blacks as compared to whites.

Chapter 7

THE REGIONAL VARIATION OF SUICIDE AND HOMICIDE BY DIFFERENT METHODS

Durkheim (1897) argued that societal suicide rates were a function of both the degree of social integration in the society and the degree of social regulation. In modern societies, it appears that where social integration is low and social regulation is weak, then suicide rates are high (Johnson, 1965). This hypothesis has been confirmed by univariate studies of such variables as the divorce rate (Stack, 1981b) and church attendance (Breault, 1986).

In the course of an examination of the regional variation of suicide rates by different methods over the continental states of America in 1980, a factor analysis identified three independent factors (using SPSSX's principal components extraction and varimax rotation). The results are shown in Table 7.1. It can be seen that suicide rates by hanging, cutting, jumping, and other methods loaded strongly on Factor I, suicide by non-domestic gas and drowning loaded strongly on Factor II, and firearms and poisoning by solids and liquids loaded strongly on Factor III.

Table 7.1 Results of the factor-analysis of the suicide rates by different methods* over the 48 continental states of America, 1980

	Factor		
	I	II	III
E950 solids and liquids	0.29	0.34	0.84#
E952 other gases and vapors	0.24	0.73#	0.02
E953 hanging, strangulation	0.77#	0.29	-0.06
E954 submersion (drowning)	0.01	0.74#	-0.03
$955 firearms and explosives	-0.20	-0.40	0.84#
E956 cutting and piercing	0.60#	0.13	0.12
E957 jumping	0.60#	0.29	0.02
E958 other methods	0.79#	-0.27	-0.04
% of variance	31.7	18.2	14.6

high loading
* not all methods had sufficient numbers so that meaningful state rates could be calculated (E951 and E959)

These results raised the question of whether there would be different regional correlates of suicide rates by each method, and the present study was designed to explore this using the data set described in Chapter 2 for the continental states of America in 1980.

Results

The total suicide rate was significantly associated with scores on Factors II (social disintegration) and III (age) (see Table 7.2). However, looking at the correlates of the factor scores with the rates of suicide by each method, it can be seen that only suicide by firearms/explosives has the same pattern of correlations as the total suicide rate. Indeed, only suicide by firearms/explosive and by solids/liquids correlated with scores on Factor II (social disintegration).

Table 7.2 Results of the factor analysis and the correlations of the factor scores with the suicide and homicide rates

	Factor						
	I	II	III	IV	V	VI	VII
Suicide							
solids/liquids	0.27*	0.64*	-0.04	-0.08	-0.03	-0.02	0.20
gases/vapors	0.26*	0.11	0.01	-0.49*	0.45*	0.06	0.20
hanging	0.43*	-0.03	0.20	-0.58*	0.15	-0.15	0.34*
drowning	0.08	0.03	0.43*	-0.06	0.07	0.16	0.29*
firearms/explosives	-0.33*	0.75*	-0.33*	0.13	-0.12	-0.09	-0.20
cutting/piercing	0.34*	0.22	0.03	-0.21	0.03	-0.02	0.29*
jumping	0.55*	0.10	0.29*	-0.05	0.13	0.09	0.04
other methods	0.43*	0.10	0.17	-0.10	0.11	-0.10	0.09
total suicide rate	-0.02	0.85*	-0.24*	-0.11	-0.03	-0.07	-0.04
Homicide							
hanging	0.49*	0.52*	-0.11	0.17	-0.11	0.08	0.09
firearms	0.04	0.30*	-0.07	0.75*	-0.35*	0.08	-0.23
cutting/piercing	0.49*	0.22	-0.03	0.59*	-0.22	0.04	-0.07
other	0.32*	0.35*	-0.06	0.42*	-0.46*	0.15	0.11
total homicide rate	0.18	0.29*	-0.07	0.73*	-0.37*	0.10	-0.17

* significant at the 5% level or better

Labels:

Factor I	urban/wealth	Factor V	labor force disintegration
Factor II	social disintegration	Factor VI	unemployment
Factor III	age	Factor VII	Roman Catholic
Factor IV	southern		

Considering all the different methods, significant correlations were obtained with each of the factor scores except for Factor VI. The factor with the most significant correlations was Factor I (urban/wealth) with positive correlations for suicide by solids/liquids, gases/vapors, hanging, cutting/piercing, jumping and other methods and a negative correlation for suicide by firearms/explosives.

Homicide Rates

A similar analysis was carried out for homicide rates by different methods. State data were available for homicide rates by hanging/strangulation, firearms, cutting and piercing instruments, and all other methods. The correlations between these separate homicide rates and the seven factor scores based on the set of social variables is shown in Table 7.2.

It can be seen that only homicide by firearms produced exactly the same pattern as the total homicide rate, that is, significant correlations with scores on Factors II (social disintegration), IV (southern), and V (labor force participation). In contrast, homicide rates by hanging/strangulation correlated with scores on Factors I (urban/wealth) and II (social disintegration), while homicide rates by cutting and piercing instruments correlated with scores on Factors I (urban/wealth) and IV (southern). Homicide rates by the residual category, all other methods, produced a similar pattern of correlations to that for homicide by firearms except for an additional association with scores on Factor I (urban/wealth).

The major finding in this analysis, then, was the presence of moderate correlations between homicide rates by methods other than firearms with scores on the factor assessing urban/wealth (Factor I).

Discussion

Durkheim predicted that where social integration and regulation were weak, suicide should be more common. The present study has indicated that this is true only for suicide committed by firearms/explosives and by solids/liquids. Suicide by other methods was not related to scores on a cluster of variables that appear to measure a lack of social integration (divorce, interstate migration, church attendance, crime rates, and alcohol consumption).

Clarke and Lester (1989) have proposed that the rate of suicide by particular methods of suicide might be affected by the availability of particular method for suicide. For example, suicide by car exhaust was more common in states with more cars per capita, and suicide by firearm was more common in states with higher levels of gun ownership. Such factors may have affected some of the correlations reported here.

However, suicide by hanging and cutting is less likely to be affected by regional differences in the availability of particular methods for suicide. Knives and ropes/sheets are easily obtained. Thus, Durkheim's theory should be subject to fewer alternative influences for such methods of suicide.

It must be concluded that explanations of the regional variation in suicide rates will need additional concepts beyond Durkheim's to explain the different patterns found for each method of suicide.

The association between "southerness" and homicide rates appears to be reasonably robust, holding true for homicide by firearms, cutting and piercing instruments, and all other methods. However, homicide by methods other than firearms does show an additional social correlate, namely with scores on the urban/wealth factor.

Chapter 8

STABILITY AND CHANGES OVER TIME

Two further issues are raised by the study reported in Chapter 2. First, are these patterns of social variables found for years other than 1980, and do they correlate in a similar fashion with rates of suicide and homicide? Second, are changes in these social characteristics over time related to changes in the rates of suicide and homicide over the same time period? The present study was designed to answer both of these questions. Social characteristics for the states of America will be examined for 1970 and 1980, their pattern of associations explored and their association with rates of suicide and homicide calculated, and the relationship between changes in these social characteristics and changes in the suicide and homicide rates examined.

A subset of social variables from those used in Chapter 2 were chosen for this study: the unemployment rate, the divorce rate, the percentage of black citizens, the birth rate, the percent of residents born abroad, the percent of urban population, the median age, the per capita personal income, the percentage of persons not moving house in the previous five years, the overall crime rate, and the population.

Results

The sets of data for 1970 and for 1980 were factor analyzed using a principal components extraction with a varimax rotation to produce orthogonal (independent) factors. For both 1970 and for 1980 four factors were identified (see Table 8.1). Factor I in both years had high loadings from the percentage of urban population and per capita income. Factor II in both years had high loadings from age. Factor III in both years had high loadings from divorce rates and migration. These three factors were similar to those identified in Chapter 2. Factor IV differs slightly in the two years. In both years, unemployment was loaded on the factor, but the percentage of black citizens was associated in opposite directions in the two years, suggesting that the pattern of unemployment changed dramatically between 1970 and 1980.

The association between the factor scores and rates of suicide and homicide are shown in Table 8.1. (The associations between the individual social characteristics and the rates of suicide and homicide are shown in Table 8.2.) In both 1970 and 1980, suicide rates were associated strongly with

Factor III scores, again confirming that suicide rates are associated with social integration as Durkheim proposed.

Table 8.1 Results of the factor analysis of the social variables in 1970 and 1980 (decimal points omitted) and correlations between factor scores and rates of suicide and homicide

	1970				1980			
	I	II	III	IV	I	II	III	IV
unemployment	15	27	-04	80#	-01	15	02	75#
divorce rate	07	05	89#	07	01	-06	95#	02
percent black	08	55#	-20	-62#	01	-04	-14	78#
birth rate	-11	89#	20	05	-12	-93#	19	-15
foreign born	77#	-36	-15	25	87#	28	-03	-07
percent urban	89#	-06	18	07	91#	-01	13	-01
median age	25	-85#	-06	-15	26	92#	-06	-02
personal income	78#	-42#	06	11	75#	30	10	-34
(no) migration	-06	-11	-92#	01	-17	38	-77#	36
crime rate	85#	10	39	08	77#	06	51#	06
population	76#	-02	-22	-31	72#	05	-28	34
Correlation with								
suicide rate	0.04	0.07	0.78*	0.21	0.03	-0.18	0.82*	-0.16
homicide rate	0.18	0.57*	0.12	-0.57*	0.28	-0.09	0.30*	0.67*

high factor loading (> 0.40)
* significant at the 5% level or better

In both years too, homicide rates were associated with the percent of black citizens. However, the secondary associations differed in the two years. In 1970 homicide rates were associated with the factor tapping age, whereas in 1980 homicide rates were associated with the factors tapping urbanization and social integration.

Looking at changes in the variables (see Table 8.2), the results differed depending on whether absolute changes or percentage changes were examined. For absolute changes, changes in income, migration rates and the population were associated with changes in the suicide rates. For percentage changes, divorce rates and migration rates were associated with changes in the suicide rate.

Absolute changes in the homicide rate were associated with changes in income, population and foreign born population. Percentage changes in the homicide rate were associated with changes in the unemployment rate and the crime rate.

Discussion

On the whole the temporal stability of the patterns of association between the social characteristics of the states and the associations between these characteristics and rates of suicide and homicide are noteworthy. For example, divorce rates and migration rates in the states are consistently associated with each other and with the rate of suicide. Similarly, the percentage of blacks and population size are consistently related to homicide rates.

Table 8.2 Pearson correlations between the social variables (and changes in them) and suicide and homicide rates

	Suicide				Homicide			
	1970	1980	absolute change	percent change	1970	1980	absolute change	percent change
unemployment	0.11	-0.11	0.14	0.05	-0.08	0.23	-0.19	-0.27*
divorce	0.71*	0.78*	0.13	0.29*	0.17	0.40*	-0.18	0.10
% black	-0.34*	-0.30*	-0.18	-0.01	0.85*	0.68*	-0.04	-0.08
birth rate	0.26*	0.34*	-0.21	-0.11	0.39*	-0.01	0.08	0.01
foreign born	-0.06	0.01	-0.18	0.15	-0.25*	0.16	0.45*	-0.23
% urban	0.13	0.08	-0.08	-0.04	0.07	0.29*	-0.07	-0.09
median age	-0.17	-0.19	0.19	0.11	-0.20	0.02	-0.14	-0.13
income	0.08	0.04	-0.42*	0.03	-0.24	-0.09	0.34*	0.05
(no) migration	-0.74*	-0.79*	0.35*	0.32*	-0.20	-0.08	-0.09	-0.04
crime rate	0.35*	0.42*	-0.18	0.11	0.26*	0.35*	0.22	0.25*
population	-0.12	-0.19	-0.25*	-0.21	0.25*	0.42*	0.26*	-0.03

* significant at the 5% level or better

Correlates of changes in the suicide and homicide rates, however, are quite different. First of all, the correlates are different depending upon whether absolute or percentage changes are examined. Second, the significant social correlates of changing rates of suicide and homicide are different from those of the rates in one year.

There are exceptions. Divorce is correlated with the suicide rate of the states, and in addition percentage changes in the divorce rate are associated with changes in the suicide rate. Thus, divorce appears to be a powerful correlate of suicide rates. Divorce can be seen as affecting the degree of social integration in a society, and so its associations with suicide in the present study can be seen as powerful support for Durkheim's theory of suicide. The crime rate is a powerful correlate of homicide rates in a similar fashion.

Chapter 9

SOCIAL CORRELATES OF PSYCHOSOMATIC AND ACCIDENTAL DEATHS

Several studies have explored the relationship between death rates from suicide and homicide and death rates from other causes. Field (1963) added the suicide and homicide rates together to derive a measure of the general aggressiveness of a society, and he subtracted the rates to derive a measure of anger-in versus anger-out. He found that the general aggressiveness measure correlated positively with the rates of death from motor vehicle accidents while the anger-out measure correlated positively with the rate of death from hypertension and negatively with the rate of death from ulcers.

The present study was undertaken to explore how the rates of deaths from two psychosomatic diseases (ulcers and asthma) varied with the the social characteristics of the states of America using the methodology and the data set described in Chapter 2. Would the social correlates be similar or different from those found for suicide and homicide in previous studies? For comparison purposes, rates of death from cirrhosis of the liver and from motor vehicle accidents (two indirectly self-destructive causes of death), two major medical causes of death (malignant neoplasms and cardiovascular disorders) and of suicide and homicide were also studied.

Results

In Table 9.1, it can be seen that Factor II (social disintegration) was correlated significantly with the suicide rate. In addition, this factor also correlated significantly with the indirectly self-destructive behaviors of death from motor vehicle accidents and chronic liver disease/cirrhosis.

Furthermore, deaths from chronic liver disease/cirrhosis were higher in the urban/wealthy states (Factor I) and in states with an older population (Factor III). Deaths from motor vehicle accidents were lower in these states.

Deaths from ulcers and asthma had few correlates. Deaths from ulcers were associated with factor scores on Factor III (age structure), while deaths from asthma were associated only with factor scores from Factor VI (unemployment).

Deaths from homicide were associated with southernness (Factor IV), social disintegration (Factor II), and participation in the labor force (Factor V).

The two natural causes of death included in the study, cardiovascular diseases and malignant neoplasms, both correlated strongly with scores on

Factor III. Factor III had high loadings from age-related variables and so seems to measure the age structure of the states. States with more elderly and fewer young people have high rates of death from cardiovascular diseases and malignant neoplasms.

Table 9.1 Correlations between factor scores and death rates from selected causes

	Factor						
	I	II	III	IV	V	VI	VII
suicide	-0.02	0.85*	-0.24	-0.11	-0.03	-0.07	-0.04
homicide	0.18	0.29*	-0.07	0.73*	-0.37*	0.10	-0.17
liver dis./cirrhosis	0.59*	0.27*	0.38*	0.04	-0.11	0.24	0.11
motor vehicles	-0.31*	0.54*	-0.45	0.01	-0.20	-0.29*	-0.16
ulcers	0.05	-0.14	0.36*	-0.14	-0.13	-0.08	0.06
asthma	-0.07	0.13	-0.11	-0.22	-0.14	-0.27*	-0.23
cardiovascular dis.	-0.17	-0.37*	0.71*	-0.16	-0.36*	-0.03	-0.12
mal. neoplasms	0.05	-0.16	0.87*	0.04	-0.34*	0.07	0.06

Labels:

I	urban/wealth	V	labor force participation		
II	social disintegration	VI	unemployment		
III	age	VII	Roman Catholicism	IV	southern

* significant at the 5% level or better

Discussion

The present study has shown that deaths from motor vehicle accidents and from chronic liver disease and cirrhosis in the continental states of America are associated in the same way as deaths from suicide with indices of the level of social disintegration in the states. Deaths from motor vehicle accidents and from chronic liver disease and cirrhosis are associated in opposite directions from each other with indices of urban/wealth and age structure. These results suggest that deaths from motor vehicle accidents and from chronic liver disease and cirrhosis may reflect self-destructive tendencies, tendencies which manifest themselves differently in urban versus rural locales and in locales with older versus younger populations. In the present data set, the suicide rate of the states was related to the death rate from chronic liver disease/cirrhosis (Pearson $r = 0.23$) and from motor vehicle accidents ($r = 0.64$). Incidentally, although the category of deaths from chronic liver disease/cirrhosis includes deaths from etiological causes other than alcohol abuse, the death rates from chronic liver disease and cirrhosis and the average alcohol consumption of the states were significantly associated (Pearson $r = 0.44$).

Death rates from ulcers and asthma appeared to have few social correlates. It may be that these causes of death are less strongly related to sociocultural variables, or it may be that they are not strongly related to the particular sociocultural indicators chosen for the present study. Further research on this issue would help decide between these two alternatives.

Chapter 10

SUICIDE AND HOMICIDE IN RURAL AMERICA

Kowalski, Faupel and Starr (1987) studied the association of social variables with suicide rates in 3108 counties in the USA. Of eighteen social variables examined, seven were associated with suicide rates, including divorce rates, the percentage of people living alone, migration, median family income, income inequality, education, and urbanization. However, when they examined these associations for urban and rural counties separately, the significant associations were found only for urban counties. The suicide rates of rural counties were found to be unassociated with these social variables.

This raises the question of what social variables might be associated with rural suicide rates, if any. The present study differs from Kowalski's in looking for social correlates of rural suicide rates *and* urban suicide rates *within* each region, rather than looking at the influence of the percentage of urban versus rural residents in a region on the suicide rate or looking at the associations between social variables and the suicide rate in relatively urban regions versus relatively rural regions.

To achieve consistency between Census classifications and mortality statistics, the definition of rural was towns with populations of 10,000 or less since the mortality data did not identify separately the deaths for towns with populations less than 2,500 (the usual definition).

Results

Urban and rural suicide rates were not significantly associated over the states of America (Pearson $r = 0.16$), whereas urban and rural homicides were ($r = 0.551$, $p < 0.001$). Thus, states with high urban homicide rates also had high rural homicide rates.

Urban suicide rates were significantly lower than rural suicide rates in the states (means 10.54 and 17.13, standard deviations 3.67 and 7.28; $t = 6.01$, $df = 47$, two-tailed $p < 0.001$), while urban and rural homicide rates were not significantly different (means 8.72 and 9.18, standard deviations 5.07 and 6.65; $t = 0.56$, $df = 47$).

The association between the factor scores and the rates of urban and rural suicide and homicide are shown in Table 10.1. It can be seen that the social correlates of urban suicide rates were somewhat different from the social correlates of rural suicide rates. Urban suicide rates were associated with scores on Factor II (social disintegration) and Factor IV (southern). Urban suicide rates were higher in states where social disintegration was greater and which were less southern.

Table 10.1 Correlations between social factor scores and urban and rural rates of suicide and homicide and results of the multiple regressions

Pearson Correlations	urban suicide	rural suicide	urban homicide	rural homicide
Factor I	-0.16	0.47*	0.17	0.18
Factor II	0.67*	0.56*	0.19	0.55*
Factor III	-0.11	-0.12	-0.07	-0.01
Factor IV	-0.33*	0.14	0.61*	0.59*
Factor V	-0.05	-0.01	-0.35*	-0.37*
Factor VI	-0.08	-0.05	0.18	-0.12
Factor VII	0.05	0.13	-0.26*	0.09

* significant at the 5% level or better

Factor I	urban/wealth	Factor II	social disintegration
Factor III	age	Factor IV	southern
Factor V	labor force participation	Factor VI	unemployment
Factor VII	Roman Catholic		

In contrast, rural suicide rates were associated with scores on Factor I (urban/wealth) and Factor II (social disintegration). Thus, rural suicide rates were higher in the more urban/wealthy states and in those states where indices of social disintegration were higher.

The social correlates of urban and rural homicide rates were somewhat similar. Urban homicides rates were associated with scores on Factor IV (southern), Factor V (labor force participation) and Factor VII (Roman Catholic). Rural homicide rates were associated also with scores on Factor IV and Factor V, but also with scores on Factor II (social disintegration).

The association between rural suicide rates and the percentage of urban residents in a state merits further exploration. The percentage of the population living in urban areas in a state was not associated with the urban suicide rate (Pearson $r = -0.16$) but it was associated positively with the rural suicide rate ($r = 0.57$, one-tailed $p < 0.001$). Thus, in states where the rural population was relatively smaller in percentage terms, the rural suicide rate was relatively greater.

Discussion

The results of the present study on the suicide rates in urban and rural America by state supports Durkheim's theory of suicide for both urban and rural America. In both rural and urban America, when social disintegration was stronger, suicide rates were higher. However, rural suicide rates were higher in states which were more urban and wealthier while urban suicide rates were higher in the less southern states.

Homicide rates were higher in both urban and rural areas in the more southern states of America. This supports the theory that the southern states of America are characterized by a violent subculture (Gastil, 1971). However, interestingly, rural homicide rates were related to indices of social disintegration in the same way that rural suicide rates were, indicating that Henry and Short's theory might well not apply to rural America. Henry and Short hypothesized that suicide and homicide are alternate behaviors and that, where one behavior is relatively more common, the other behavior would be relatively less common. This appears not to be the case for rural America.

The Correlations In Urban And Rural States

Kowalski, et al. (1987) examined the social correlates, not of urban and rural suicide and homicide rates in different regions, but rather of the suicide and homicide rates in urban and rural regions. They found social correlates of suicide rates only for urban counties, not for rural counties. To check upon their findings, the 48 continental states were divided by a median split into the more and less rural (using 67 percent of the population living in urban areas as the median). The correlations between the social factor scores and the suicide and homicide rates in the more rural and the less rural states are shown in Table 10.2.

Table 10.2 Social correlates of suicide and homicide rates in urban and rural states

	urban states		rural states	
	suicide rates	homicide rates	suicide rates	homicide rates
Factor I	-0.32	0.07	0.06	-0.37*
Factor II	0.91***	0.40*	0.59***	0.06
Factor III	-0.25	-0.05	-0.15	-0.09
Factor IV	-0.08	0.54**	-0.24	0.88***
Factor V	-0.10	-0.36*	0.24	-0.35*
Factor VI	-0.13	-0.19	-0.02	0.33
Factor VII	-0.05	-0.26	-0.07	-0.16

* significant at the 5% level or better

Factor I	urban/wealth	Factor II	social disintegration
Factor III	age	Factor IV	southern
Factor V	labor force participation	Factor VI	unemployment
Factor VII	Roman Catholic		

Social disintegration scores (Factor II) correlated significantly with the suicide rates for both the more and the less rural states. "Southerness" (Factor IV) and labor-force participation (Factor V) correlated significantly with the homicide rates for both the more and the less rural states. Social disintegration scores (Factor II) correlated with the homicide rates only in the less rural states while urban/wealth scores (Factor I) correlated with homicide rates only in the more rural states.

Thus, the finding by Kowalksi, et al. that social correlates of suicide rates are found only in urban counties, was not replicated. The present analyses found that the social correlates of both suicide and homicide rates were similar in both urban and rural regions.

Chapter 11

THE SEASONALITY OF SUICIDE

Abe, et al. (1986) reported that the degree of seasonal variation in suicide and the gross national product per capita were negatively related in Japan over the period 1900-1982. The present chapter examined this association over the continental states of America in 1980.

The seasonal variation in suicide for each state was calculated by computing the chi-square statistic for the monthly suicide totals in each state and converting this to a contingency coefficient to control for the number of suicides. The gross state product per capita for each state was obtained from Renshaw, et al. (1988).

The Pearson correlation between the two variables was 0.02 (not statistically significant). Thus, the result of Abe, et al. does not appear to generalize to the regional variation in the seasonality of suicide over the continental states of America.

To explore the correlates of the seasonality in suicide rates further, the seasonality index was correlated with the factor scores obtained in Chapter 2 from the factor-analysis of the set of social variables. The results are shown in Table 11.1. The seasonality of suicide was greater in the less urban/wealthy states (Factor I), the less southern states (Factor VI), and the more Roman Catholic states (Factor VII).

Thus, though the seasonality of suicide does have social correlates, they are not similar to those suggested by Abe, et al. (1986).

Table 11.1 Correlates of the seasonal variation of suicide

		Pearson r
Factor I	urban/wealth	-0.39*
Factor II	social disintegration	-0.06
Factor III	age	-0.21
Factor IV	southern	-0.38*
Factor V	labor force participation	-0.03
Factor VI	unemployment	-0.20
Factor VII	Roman Catholicism	0.34*

* significant at the 5% level or better

Chapter 12

POCKETS OF VIOLENCE

The relationship between suicide rates and homicide rates has puzzled researchers for a long time (Lester, 1987b). In the sociological theory of Henry and Short (1954), suicide and homicide are opposed behaviors. Among the oppressed, for example blacks in America and South Africa, homicide rates are high and suicide rates low, whereas among the oppressors (whites) suicide rates are high and homicide rates low (Lester, 1971). Henry and Short also argued that different experiences of punishment led to the development of assaultive/homicidal tendencies and the development of depressed/suicidal tendencies.

A large number of regional studies of correlates of homicide rates or of suicide rates have appeared, but in general homicide rates do not vary consistently in the opposite direction from suicide rates with target societal variables (Lester, 1987b).

Assuming that the rate of suicide and homicide are only weakly associated or not associated over a set of regions (the correlation was 0.24 [p = 0.053] for the continental states of America in 1980), this raises the possibility of comparing regions with different combinations of high and low rates of each method of violence. Some regions will be high in both types of aggression (homicide and suicide), some low in both types of aggression and some high in only one type of aggression. How do these communities differ?

Humphrey and Kupferer (1977) explored this question using counties in North Carolina. Comparing the counties high in both types of violence and those low in both types, they found that the counties high in both types of violence had fewer blacks, a lower migration rate, less unemployment, fewer poor people and more intact families. Lester (1985) compared cities in America. He found that cities high in both types of violence had high crime rates and more poor people and were in the south and middle of America; cities with only high suicide rates had low rates of violent crime, high rates of property crime, and less poverty and tended to be in the west and north of America; cities high only in homicide had high rates of violent crime and low rates of property crime, more poverty and tended to be in the north and east of America; and cities low in both types of violence had low crime rates, less poverty and were in the north and middle of America.

The present study was designed to explore the variation of societal variables with violence using this method of classifying regions - into those high and low in homicide and suicide - using the states of America and a more complex analysis of the social characteristics of the regions, the factor analysis of social variables described in Chapter 2.

Results And Discussion

The classification of the states into those high and low in suicide and homicide rates is shown in Table 12.1. The results of the comparison of these four types of states on the seven factor scores are shown in Table 12.2. Several clear differences can be observed.

Violent States: Those states high in both suicide and homicide were very high in social disintegration (Factor II), high in southernness (Factor IV), and moderately low in unemployment (Factor VI).

Nonviolent States: States low in both suicide and homicide were very low in social disintegration, low in southernness, and low in unemployment.

Inwardly Violent States: Those states high in suicide and low in homicide were moderately high in social disintegration, very low in southernness, and average in unemployment.

Outwardly Violent States: Those states high in homicide and low in suicide were moderately low in social disintegration, very high in southernness, and very high in unemployment.

Table 12.1 Classification of the states

	low suicide low homicide	low suicide high homicide	high suicide low homicide	high suicide high homicide
	CT	AL	CO	AZ
	IA	AR	DE	CA
	KS	IL	ID	FL
	MA	IN	ME	GA
	MN	MD	MT	KY
	NE	MI	OR	LA
	NH	MS	SD	NV
	NJ	MO	UT	NM
	ND	NY	VT	OK
	OH	NC	WV	TN
	PA	SC	WY	TX
	RI			VA
	WI			WA
mean rates:				
suicide	10.4	10.6	13.8	14.5
homicide	4.8	12.0	5.2	13.0

Table 12.2 Differences between the four types of regions on one-way analyses of variance. (Scores are normalized z-scores, with standard deviations shown in parentheses)

Factor	low S low H	low S high H	high S low H	high S high H	F
I	0.29	-0.17	-0.46	0.24	1.55
	(0.84)	(1.20)	(0.76)	(1.07)	
II	-0.73	-0.36	0.36	0.72	8.04*
	(0.56)	(0.39)	(0.78)	(1.25)	
III	0.48	0.08	-0.47	-0.14	2.05
	(0.51)	(0.52)	(1.57)	(0.94)	
IV	-0.61	0.77	-0.70	0.55	11.53*
	(0.49)	(1.01)	(0.69)	(0.84)	
V	0.31	-0.06	0.18	-0.41	1.30
	(0.63)	(1.03)	(0.98)	(1.23)	
VI	-0.46	0.70	0.17	-0.27	3.71*
	(0.81)	(1.12)	(1.02)	(0.75)	
VII	0.25	-0.12	0.20	-0.31	0.89
	(1.23)	(0.56)	(1.04)	(0.94)	

Labels:

I	urban/wealth	V	labor force participation
II	social disintegration	VI	unemployment
III	age	VII	Roman Catholicism
IV	southern		

* significant at the 5% level or better

Thus, it appears that the four types of states differ in their social characteristics. To identify one representative state from each group would distort the wide variation within each group but would serve to provide a concrete example of each type of state. Nonviolent - Connecticut; Violent - Nevada; Inwardly violent - Oregon; and Outwardly violent - Alabama.

An interesting geographical variation appeared in this study. The total amount of violence (of whatever kind) showed a north-south variation (Factor IV), whereas the direction in which aggression was expressed (suicide versus homicide) showed an east-west variation (longitude is loaded on Factor II, see Chapter 2). Whitt, et al. (1972) have suggested that these two measures (the total lethal aggression rate and the direction in which it is expressed) may be more useful in empirical studies than suicide and homicide rates (see Chapter 4).

The methodology of the present study was, in some ways, more complex than typical regional studies of suicide and homicide rates which usually seek simple correlates of just suicide rates or just homicide rates. The present study factor analyzed the social variables to identify the major social dimensions on which the regions differ. Then also, the realization that suicide and homicide rates are rarely strongly correlated permitted an examination of the four possible combinations of high and low rates of suicide and homicide.

Part Two: International Comparisons

Chapter 13

A COMPARISON OF SRI LANKA AND THE USA

The findings reported in Chapter 2 for the social correlates of the suicide and homicide rates of the states of America have some interest for social scientists. But ideally, social scientists would like to explain the regional variation of suicide and homicide rates in general, not merely in the USA. Social scientists would be less enthusiastic about Durkheim's theory of suicide, for example, if it explained the regional variation of suicide rates only in the USA and not in other countries. Therefore, it is important to replicate the findings reported in Chapter 2 using other countries.

The present chapter reports a study of suicide rates in the districts of Sri Lanka. A set of social characteristics for which data are available for Sri Lanka are factor-analysed, as in the study reported in Chapter 2, and scores for these factor correlated with the suicide rates of the districts. In addition, a smaller subset of variables common both to the present Sri Lankan study and the earlier study of the USA will be analysed to provide a direct comparison of the relevance of one set of variables to regional variation in suicide rates in two countries.

Method

Data for Sri Lanka were available for 1971. Kearney and Miller (1983, 1985) provided data for the suicide rate of each of the 22 districts, the population density, the population increase from 1963-1971, the number of males per 100 females, the participation of males and females in the labor force, the literacy of males and females, the age at marriage for females, and the male and female unemployment rates. Langford (1981) provided data for the population and the birth rate. The Department of Census and Statistics (1978) provided data for the percentage of urban population, the net migration rate for 1963-1971, the percentage of Tamils (Sri Lanka has a Sinhalese majority and a Tamil minority) and the overall literacy rate.

Results

The correlations between the suicide rates in the twenty-two districts of Sri Lanka and the social indicators are shown in Table 13.1. Suicide rates were positively associated with the population increase, the sex ratio, male participation in the labor force, the birth rate, inter-district migration and the percentage of Tamils and negatively associated with the population, the population density, male and female unemployment rates and the age of females at marriage. Literacy, urbanization and female participation in the labor force were not related to the suicide rates.

Table 13.1 Correlations between social indicators and rates of personal violence and the results of a factor analysis for Sri Lanka

	Pearson r	Factor Analysis		
	suicide rate	I	II	III
population	-0.42*	-0.26	0.85#	-0.03
population density	-0.48*	-0.37	0.86#	-0.02
population increase	0.44*	0.94#	-0.26	0.01
sex ratio	0.49**	0.92#	-0.13	0.10
labor force participation:				
males	0.49**	0.81#	-0.25	0.23
females	-0.29	-0.49#	-0.03	-0.59#
unemployment males	-0.66***	-0.58#	0.66#	-0.32
females	-0.64***	-0.64#	0.61#	-0.31
age at marriage	-0.51**	-0.75#	0.45#	-0.40#
birth rate	0.42*	0.62#	-0.51	0.42#
urban population	-0.09	0.13	0.72#	0.61#
inter-district migration	0.38*	0.95#	-0.04	-0.11
percentage of Tamils	0.57**	-0.07	-0.27	0.88#
literacy	-0.10	-0.04	0.72#	-0.22
percent of variance		55.7%	15.7%	11.4%
Pearson correlation with total suicide rate		0.38*	-0.35	0.34

* one-tailed $p < 0.05$
** one-tailed $p < 0.01$
*** one-tailed $p < 0.001$
# high loading (> 0.40)

Sri Lanka Versus The USA

The comparison of eight similar social indicators in accounting for suicide rates in regions of the USA and Sri Lanka are shown in Table 13.2. The data for the USA parallel the Sri Lankan data except that the interstate migration is for a five-year rather than an eight year period. In addition, the percentage of blacks was used as an ethnic indicator in place of the percentage of Tamils.

For Sri Lanka, the suicide rate was correlated negatively with population size, population density, and male unemployment, positively with inter-district migration, the birth rate and the percentage of Tamils, and not correlated with female labor force participation or the percentage of the population in urban areas (see Table 13.2). For the USA, the suicide rate was correlated negatively with the percentage of blacks and population density, positively with interstate migration and the birth rate, and not correlated with the participation of females in the labor force, population size and the male unemployment rate (see Table 13.2). These two sets of correlations are similar for population density (both negative), female participation in the labor force (both not significant), the birth rate (both positive), the percentage of the urban population (both not significant), and migration (both positive). In addition, both countries had an association between ethnicity and suicide rates: the higher the proportion of Tamils in a district and the higher the proportion of whites in a state the higher the suicide rate. Thus there is agreement for six of the eight variables.

Table 13.2 Results of the factor analyses for the USA and Sri Lanka

	USA				Sri Lanka			
	I	II	III	Pearson r	I	II	III	Pearson r
percent minority	-0.49	0.14	0.08	-0.30*	-0.13	0.02	0.94#	0.57*
birth rate	0.14	-0.87#	0.01	0.34*	-0.49	0.63#	0.36	0.42*
% urban population	0.17	0.12	0.93#	0.08	0.79#	0.36	0.43	-0.09
migration	0.62#	-0.54	-0.04	0.80*	-0.21	0.88#	-0.25	0.38*
male unemployment	-0.70#	0.11	0.06	-0.10	0.69#	-0.50	-0.35	-0.66*
females labor force	0.79#	0.20	0.10	0.08	-0.02	-0.70#	-0.45	-0.29
population	-0.46	0.13	0.74#	-0.19	0.90#	-0.20	-0.14	-0.42*
population density	0.05	0.80#	0.37	-0.50*	0.92#	-0.29	-0.12	-0.48*
percent variance	32.5%	20.9%	13.6%		49.1%	23.1%	13.4%	
Pearson correlation with suicide rate	0.32*	-0.59*	0.06		-0.41*	0.29	0.41*	

high loading
* one-tailed $p < 0.05$ or better

The patterns identified by the factor analysis (a PC extraction with varimax rotation using SPSSX) are a little different (see Table 13.2). Each analysis identified three factors. For Sri Lanka, the factors may be labelled dense and urban (Factor I), high migration (Factor II), and ethnicity (Factor II).

For the USA, Factor I appears to be similar to the second and third factors for Sri Lanka. For the USA, Factors II and III appear to be different aspects of the first factor for Sri Lanka and may be labelled densely populated and urban respectively.

Thus, the results of the factor analysis are not quite similar for the two countries. However, the correlations of the factors with the suicide rates are similar. The first USA factor was seen as similar to the second and third Sri Lankan factors, and all correlated positively with suicides rates. The second and third USA factors were seen as similar to the first Sri Lankan factor, and two of the three correlated negatively with suicide rates.

Discussion

The present paper has conducted a regional analysis of suicide in two countries of the world and presented the rates of comparable analyses for the two countries. Both sets of analyses (in Sri Lanka and the USA) indicated that the social characteristics of regions are powerful predictors of the suicide rates of the regions. Furthermore, some of the social characteristics were related in an identical fashion to suicide rates in both countries, population density and inter-region migration for example.

It was perhaps too much to be hoped for that the factor analyses of a set of social characteristics in both countries would be identical. However, the results of the factor analyses had some elements in common and had comparable (if not identical) correlations with the suicide rates of the regions.

In particular, Factor I for the USA and Factor II for Sri Lanka both seem to tap lack of social integration, with loadings on inter-region migration. Thus, Durkheim's hypothesis that social integration is an important sociological determinant of regional suicide rates is supported.

This study is important because it moves the study of social characteristics which might relate to the suicide rates of regions from the individual level to a more general level. If regional studies are to be universally relevant, the findings from one country must be shown to be generally accepted to other countries. Simultaneous study of two or more countries is, therefore, necessary to identify which findings from one country are specific to that country and which are acceptable to other countries.

The present study choose to compare the USA and Sri Lanka primarily because of the availability of data from two different nations - from the American and Asian continents. Future studies should give more consideration to the choice of nations, searching for a theoretical purpose in the comparison.

Chapter 14

A COMPARISON OF HUNGARY AND THE USA

The present study reports parallel ecological studies in the USA and Hungary similar to the study reported in Chapter 13 above in order to explore the generality of the pattern analysis presented in Chapter 2 of this book.

Method

Data for the USA were obtained from the annual publication *Statistical Abstract of the United States and the Census of the Population, 1980*. Data for Hungary were obtained from the Central Statistical Office in Budapest.

Data were obtained for seven variables for 1980: the overall crime rate, the violent crime rate, the number of divorces per 1,000 women over the age of 15, the ratio of females to males, the percentage of people aged 15-39, the percent of those aged 15-19 who did not complete elementary school, and the percentage of people aged 60-64 who did not complete elementary school.

These variables were factor analyzed using the Statistical Package for the Social Sciences (SPSSX), with a principal components extraction and a varimax rotation. Factor scores were correlated with suicide rates by means of Pearson correlations.

Results

The factor analysis of the seven social indicators for the 19 Hungarian counties identified two factors (see Table 14.1). Neither factor was associated with the suicide rate, and only one social indicator (the divorce rate) was associated with suicide rates.

The factor analysis of the seven social indicators for the 48 continental states of the USA identified three factors (see Table 14.1), two of which correlated with suicide rates. Of the seven social indicators, five correlated significantly with suicide rates: the crime rate, the divorce rate, the ratio of females to males, the percentage of young adults, and lack of education in the elderly.

Discussion

This study identified one common social correlate of regional suicide rates in Hungary and the USA. In both nations, suicides rates are higher in regions where divorce is more common. This finding can be interpreted using Durkheim's concept of social integration. Durkheim (1897) predicted that divorce leads to lower levels of social integration which in turn leads to higher suicide rates.

However, the other social indicators (such as the crime rate and ratio of females to males) which were found to correlate with suicide rates in the USA did not correlate with suicide rates in Hungary. These associations, therefore, appear to be nation-specific.

In addition, the factor analysis of the social indicators in Hungary and the USA revealed different patterns. Although Factor I for both nations had three common social indicators (the divorce rate, the ratio of females to males, and the percentage of young adults), this factor had two other components for Hungary (the crime rate and the lack of education in the elderly).

This study demonstrates again the usefulness and the importance of replicating ecological studies in several nations in order to distinguish nation-specific relationships from more general ones.

Table 14.1 Factor analysis of the social indicators for Hungary and the USA

	Hungary			USA			
	Factor I rate	**Factor II rate**	**Pearson r with suicide**	**Factor I**	**Factor II**	**Factor III**	**Pearson r with suicide**
crime rate	.63#	.20	0.07	.19	.87#	-.39	0.42*
violent crime rate	.37	.83#	0.04	-.04	.96#	-.01	0.21
divorce rate	.51#	.26	0.56*	.74	.39	.09	0.80*
females/males	-.78#	.13	0.29	-.91#	.22	.18	-0.64*
% young adults	.88#	.04	-0.09	.75#	.08	-.14	0.41*
lack of education:							
youth	-.32	.87#	0.01	-.02	-.01	.94#	-0.14
elderly	-.75#	.28	0.26	-.21	-.29	.84#	-0.29*
% of variance	40.7%	23.5%		40.4%	23.7%	18.5%	
correlation with suicide rate	-0.06	0.19		0.73*	0.29*	-0.08	

high loading (> 0.40)
* statistically significant at the 5% level or higher

Chapter 15

A COMPARISON OF ENGLAND AND THE USA

The present chapter reports a third inter-nation study of the relationship between social variables and rates of personal violence. As before in Chapters 13 and 14, it will employ the factor-analytic design of the study reported in Chapter 2 and compare the results in two nations. Thus, if the results prove reliable, the findings may have generality to more than the initial nation examined.

Method

Data on the social indicators for English counties in 1961 were obtained from the *Complete Atlas of the British Isles* (Anon, 1965). Suicide and homicide rates for 1961 were obtained from the *Statistical Review of England and Wales, 1961* (Anon, 1963). The variables studied are shown in Table 15.1.

The analyses were replicated using data for the 48 continental states of the USA in 1980. Data on the same variables as in the analysis of English counties were obtained from the volumes of the *1980 Census of the Population* and the annual volumes of the *Statistical Abstract of the United States,* both published by the United States Government Printing Office.

Results

England

The correlations between the social indicators and rates of personal violence are shown in Table 15.1. It can be seen that suicide rates of English counties were associated negatively with the size of the population, the percentage of young people, the percentage born in-county, and the birth rate and positively with the percentage of old people and the percentage of immigrants.

Homicide rates in English counties were correlated only with the percentage of people born in-county.

A factor analysis (a principal components analysis, with a varimax rotation using SPSSX) identified three factors (see Table 15.1). Factor I represents youth, Factor II low migration/immigration, and Factor III large population/densely populated. Factors I and II correlated negatively with suicide rates, but none correlated significantly with homicide rates.

America

The association of suicide and homicide rates with the social variables in America are shown in Table 15.1. It can be seen that suicide rates were correlated negatively with the population density, the percentage of elderly people, the percentage born in-state, the death rate and the infant mortality rate, and positively with the birth rate. In contrast, homicide rates were correlated positively only with the population and the infant mortality rate. The pattern of these simple bivariate correlations is quite different from that found for English counties.

Table 15.1 Correlations in England and America

	Pearson Correlations		Factor Analysis		
	suicide rate	homicide rate	I	II	III
English Counties					
population	-0.31*	-0.18	0.05	0.32	0.83#
population density	0.03	0.03	-0.02	-0.24	0.87#
% > 65 years	0.31*	0.06	-0.93#	-0.03	-0.18
% < 15 years	-0.40**	-0.05	0.85#	0.30	-0.26
% born in county	-0.33*	-0.26*	0.12	0.90#	-0.08
% immigrants	0.26*	0.01	0.11	-0.80#	0.07
average income	-0.17	0.18	0.31	-0.55#	0.45#
average patients/GP	-0.21	0.01	0.77#	-0.01	0.11
birth rate	-0.34**	0.01	0.92#	0.05	0.07
death rate	0.18	0.03	-0.87#	0.39	0.02
infant mortality	-0.23	0.16	0.16	0.80#	0.31
percent of variance			36.3%	25.8%	16.5%
correlation with:					
suicide rate			-0.34**	-0.29*	-0.14
homicide rate			-0.02	-0.10	0.01
American States					
population	-0.19	0.42**	0.62#	-0.03	0.42#
population density	-0.50**	-0.08	0.66#	0.33	0.22
% > 65 years	-0.33*	-0.18	-0.07	0.91#	-0.01
% < 15 years	0.14	0.02	-0.56#	-0.74#	0.08
% born in state	-0.68**	-0.09	-0.39	0.24	0.70#
% immigrants	0.01	0.16	0.88#	0.08	-0.11
per capita income	-0.01	-0.11	0.81#	-0.02	-0.30
average patients/GP	-0.21	-0.06	0.84#	0.15	0.03
birth rate	0.34**	-0.01	-0.45#	-0.75#	-0.19
death rate	-0.45**	-0.01	-0.03	0.92#	0.28
infant mortality	-0.37**	0.56**	0.15	0.06	0.81#
percent of variance			39.8%	23.2%	11.8%
correlation with:					
suicide rate			-0.08	-0.33**	-0.59**
homicide rate			0.15	-0.20	0.44**

high loading (> 0.40)
* one-tailed $p < 0.05$
** one-tailed $p < 0.01$

The factor analysis of the American data revealed some similarities and some differences. The factor structure was quite similar. Three factors were extracted for the USA which on the whole matched those found in England. The major difference was that the percentage of foreign born loaded on the same factor as the percentage of people born in-county for England and on the population factor in the USA.

The correlations of the factor scores with suicide and homicide rates for the USA indicated that, as in England, suicide rates were lower where there were more people born in-county/in-state. In contrast, however, suicide rates were higher in England and lower in the USA in counties/states with many older persons. For both countries, the factor of population/wealth was unrelated to suicide rates.

Whereas factor scores were not related to homicide rates in England, the percentage born in-state factor correlated positively with homicide rates in the USA.

Discussion

Examination of the results have indicated some similarities between England and the USA in both the factor pattern of social indicators and in the correlates of rates of personal violence. The eleven social variables for which data were available for both nations gave a similar factor pattern for most of the variables. The percentage of foreign-born residents loaded differently in the two nations indicating that immigrants in the two nations reside in very different types of regions. In England, immigrants appear to reside in the poorer counties, whereas in the USA immigrants appear to reside in the more populated and wealthier states. (New York and California, for example, have many immigrants.)

With regard to associations with suicide rates, the factor of population/wealth (Factor III for England and Factor I for the USA) was not associated with suicide rates in either nation, while the born-in-region factor was negatively related to suicide in both nations. This suggests that social stability, which perhaps promotes social integration, may reduce the risk of suicide.

Interestingly, the age factor (Factor I for England and Factor II for the USA) related in opposite ways to suicide in the two nations. In the USA states with a youthful population had higher suicides, while in England counties with a youthful population had lower suicide rates. The recent rise in adolescent suicide in the USA may be partly responsible for this difference.

The failure to find correlates of the homicide rate of English counties whereas correlates were found for the homicide rates of American states may reflect differences in the causation of homicide in the two nations. However, homicide rates are much lower in England than in the USA, and the low incidence of homicide in England may make the rates quite variable from year to year and of low reliability. This low reliability may preclude finding significant correlates.

The two nations in this study were examined at very different points in time - England in 1961 and the USA in 1980. It would be of interest, not only to replicate these regional studies of suicide and homicide in other nations, but also to replicate them at other time periods. In this way, we may arrive at regional correlates of rates of personal violence which have generality beyond the particular nation and the particular era chosen for a single study and which thereby contribute to a theoretical understanding of suicide. The importance, for example, of born-in-region as a correlate of suicide rates in *both* England and the USA lends *strong* support to Durkheim's (1897) proposal that social integration reduces the risk of suicide, stronger support than had the study been conducted on only one nation.

Part Three: Extensions

Chapter 16

AN INTERNATIONAL ANALOG

As we discussed in Chapter 2, two powerful sociological theories have been used to explain differences in the suicide and homicide rates of the nations of the world. Durkheim (1897) proposed that suicide rates would be higher in societies where social integration was either very strong (leading to altruistic suicide) or very weak (leading to egoistic suicide) and where social regulation was either very strong (leading to fatalistic suicide) or very weak (leading to anomic suicide). Henry and Short (1954) argued that societies where external restraints and pressures on the citizens were strong would have higher rates of homicide and lower rates of suicide, whereas societies where external restraints and pressures on the citizens were weak would have lower rates of homicide and higher rates of suicide.

These two theories have stimulated many predictions. For example, nations with high rates of divorce should have high rates or suicide (because a higher rate of divorce implies a lower level of social integration), a prediction confirmed by Stack (1980d). Or societies with totalitarian rule should have higher rates of homicide and lower rates of suicide because a higher level of totalitarianism provides a clearer external source to blame for personal unhappiness, a prediction confirmed by Lester (1981).

Indeed, a large of number of cross-national studies have correlated various social variables with national rates of suicide and homicide. Each study highlights one or two significant correlates. Stack (1981a) focussed on immigration, Lester (1974) on national indices of anxiety and extraversion, Breault and Barkey (1982) on religiosity, and Ellner (1977) on industrialization.

The purpose of the present study was to conduct one single study to explore the association of a large number of social variables with suicide and homicide rates similar to the study described in Chapter 2 on the states of America. In order to make this study comparable to the study on the states of America, a subset of the variables used in the state study was chosen for which international data were also available. Thus, the factor-analytic patterns of the variables over the states of America and over nations can be compared, as can the correlations between the factor scores and rates of suicide and homicide.

Two research strategies have been used for cross-national studies: to use data for all available nations (typically providing sample sizes of 35 to 50) and studies on more limited groups of nations. Stack (1981a), for example, studied the relationship between immigration rates and suicide rates in 34 nations, while Sainsbury, et al. (1980) limited their sample to eighteen European nations. The present study focussed on all of the nations with available data (see Table 16.1).

Table 16.1 Suicide and homicide rates of the nations per 100,000 per year in 1969-1971

	suicide	homicide		suicide	homicide
Argentina	10.0	7.3	Japan	15.1	1.3
Australia	12.7	1.5	Netherlands	7.9	0.5
Austria	23.1	1.3	Norway	8.2	0.6
Belgium	15.7	1.0	Panama	3.3	3.5
Canada	11.4	2.0	Spain	4.3	0.3
Chile	5.7	3.9	Sweden	21.5	0.9
Denmark	22.4	0.8	Syria	1.5	-
Egypt	0.0	-	Trinidad & Tobago	6.6	3.9
Finland	22.1	2.4	United Kingdom	8.1	0.8
Germany, West	21.0	1.3	USA	11.4	8.3
Ireland	2.1	0.4	Uruguay	10.3	3.7
Israel	6.2	6.2	Venezuela	6.8	7.9
			Yugoslavia	13.7	3.4

Method

The social variables for the nations are for 1970. Ratings of the gross domestic product per capita from Summers and Heston (1984), the population, the birth rate, the death rate, the percentage of children, the percentage of elderly, the population density, and the percentage of urban population from the World Bank (1984), the unemployment rate from the International Labor Office (1976), and the divorce rate from the United Nations (1984). The suicide and homicide rates were obtained for 1969-1971 from a data set established by the present author.

Results

The set of social variables was factor analyzed using SPSSX as in Chapter 2, with a principal components extraction and a varimax rotation to produce orthogonal (independent) factors.

The factor analysis of the social variables for the nations of the world resulted in three factors as did the factor analysis of similar variables for the states (see Table 16.2). However, the factor patterns were quite different.

For the nations of the world, the three factors appear to measure age structure/wealth (Factor I), size/divorce (Factor II), and the death rate

(Factor III). For the states, the three factors appear to measure the age structure (Factor I), urban/size (Factor II), and divorce/wealth (Factor III). Similarly, the correlates of suicide and homicide rates are also quite different.

Table 16.2 Factor analysis of the social variables and associations between factor scores and rates of suicide and homicide.

	Factors					
	Nations			States		
	I	II	III	I	II	III
population	-0.04	0.87#	-0.11	-0.06	0.72#	0.21
% children	-0.93#	-0.18	-0.02	0.82#	-0.41#	0.15
% elderly	0.90#	0.10	0.27	-0.86#	-0.16	0.08
% urban pop.	0.50#	0.23	-0.36	0.09	0.86#	-0.23
pop. density	0.46#	-0.13	-0.08	-0.44#	0.63#	0.10
birth rate	-0.90#	-0.15	0.10	0.81#	-0.34	-0.17
death rate	0.06	0.07	0.96#	-0.89#	-0.07	0.24
gross domestic/ state product	0.71#	0.49#	-0.28	0.35	0.31	-0.70#
divorce	0.16	0.88#	0.24	0.37	-0.04	-0.40#
unemployment	-0.65#	-0.16	-0.26	0.12	0.22	0.84#
Pearson r:						
suicide rate	0.68*	0.22	0.02	0.41*	-0.10	-0.42*
homicide rate	-0.68*	0.34	-0.50*	0.18	0.32*	0.07

high loading (> 0.40)
* significant at the 5% level or better

Table 16.3 Correlations between social variables and rates of personal violence

	Suicide		Homicide	
	nations	states	nations	states
population	0.02	-0.19	0.08	0.42*
% youth	-0.75*	0.14	0.68*	0.02
% elderly	0.70*	-0.33*	-0.64*	-0.18
% urban population	0.34*	0.08	-0.43*	0.29*
population density	0.06	-0.50*	-0.14	-0.08
birth rate	-0.72*	0.34*	0.76*	-0.01
death rate	-0.16	-0.45*	0.24	-0.01
gross domestic/state product	0.62*	0.34*	-0.55*	0.07
unemployment	-0.37*	-0.10	0.45*	0.23
divorce	0.63*	0.78*	-0.33*	0.40*

Looking at the Pearson correlations (Table 16.3), only divorce and gross domestic/state product per capita correlated similarly with suicide rates for nations and states. For homicide rates, none of the variables were associated both significantly and similarly for nations and states.

Discussion

It can be seen that the factor patterns of social variables are quite different in nations than in states, and that the associations between social variables and rates of personal violence are also quite different in nations and states.

The association of divorce with suicide rates indicates that Durkheim's (1897) focus on the importance of social integration in the etiology of social suicide rates may have some generality. However, the positive association of age with suicide rates in nations, contrasted with the negative association in states, may make it difficult for a single sociological theory to encompass all of these diverse results. It may be that different sociological theories, as well as different social variables, may be necessary to explain suicide in nations as compared to states.

Chapter 17

A TIME SERIES ANALOG

For time series analyses of data, there are specialized multiple regression packages, such as RATS, the Regression Analysis of Time Series (Doan, 1988). However, the purpose of the present chapter is to apply the factor analytic methodology of this book to a time series data set to explore the outcome.

In conducting a time series analysis, many of the variables available for an analysis over the states of America are not appropriate. For example, a measure of the extent of a southern subculture is not only unavailable by year, but also probably not meaningful if measured by year.

For the present study, data were located for six of the variables in the state data set for a time series analysis in the USA for 1945 to 1984: male participation in the labor force, female participation in the labor force, the population, the divorce rate, the unemployment rate and the birth rate. Data were obtained from the *Historical Statistics of the United States* published by the Census Bureau, supplemented by the *Statistical Abstract of the United States* published annually by the Census Bureau. (The divorce rate was expressed as a proportion of married females as in the comparison of the American and Hungarian data described in Chapter 14).

Table 17.1 Results of the factor analysis for the states of the USA

	Factor		Pearson Correlations	
	I	II	suicide rate	homicide rate
labor force				
participation: male	0.90#	0.17	0.14	-0.42*
female	0.93#	-0.03	0.08	-0.38*
population	-0.19	-0.59#	-0.19	0.42*
divorce rate	0.01	0.72#	0.80*	0.38*
unemployment rate	-0.69#	-0.17	-0.11	0.23
birth rate	0.08	0.78#	0.34*	-0.01
Pearson Correlation with:				
suicide rate	0.04	0.63*		
homicide rate	-0.45*	0.07		

The results of the factor analysis of the six variables for the states of the USA are shown in Table 17.1. As before, a PC extraction with a varimax rotation was used using SPSSX. Two factors were extracted. Factor I had loadings from participation in the labor force and unemployment, while

Factor II had loadings from the divorce rate, the birth rate and the population. Scores on Factor I were associated with homicide rates while scores on Factor II were associated with suicide rates.

The strongest single correlate of suicide rates was the divorce rate, while the strongest single correlate of homicide rates was a tie between the population and male participation in the labor force.

The factor analysis of the time series data identified only one factor which, therefore, could not be rotated. The factor scores correlated positively both with the suicide and with the homicide rate. Since the population of the USA increased each year, the population can stand for the simple time trend. The results clearly indicate that all of the variables showed a clear trend over time. (The population did indeed correlate significantly with every other variable.)

Thus, the results of this analog are not satisfactory. The period of time for which data were available had too little variation in the variables to provide a complex result for the factor analysis, and the analysis appeared to identify only simple time trends.

Table 17.2 Results of the factor analysis for the USA from 1945 to 1984

	Factor I	Pearson Correlations suicide rate	homicide rate
labor force participation:			
male	-0.96#	-0.60*	-0.83*
female	0.94#	0.36*	0.81*
population	0.94#	0.35*	0.76*
divorce rate	0.88#	0.60*	0.92*
unemployment rate	0.48#	0.76*	0.39*
birth rate	-0.92#	-0.67*	-0.89*
Pearson Correlation with:			
suicide rate	0.61*		
homicide rate	0.90*		

high loading (> 0.40)
* statistically significant at the 5% level or better

Chapter 18

A COUNTY ANALOG

In Chapter 2, the regional variation of suicide and homicide rates was studied over the continental states of America. A factor analysis of the social variables was presented, and correlations between the factors scores and the rates of personal violence examined.

It is of interest to ask whether similar results would be obtained were the study conducted over smaller regions. Two possibilities immediately come to mind based on previous ecological studies of suicide and homicide - over counties in a state and over census tracts of a city. The present chapter reports a study of counties.

The sample consisted of the twenty-one counties in New Jersey. Data were obtained for 1980 for ten social variables from the *County And City Data Book, 1983*, published by the Census Bureau (see Table 18.1). These data were subjected to a factor analysis using SPSSX, with a principal components extraction and a varimax rotation. Three factors were identified (see Table 18.1). Factor scores were then correlated with suicide and homicide rates for the counties using rates provided by the Center for Health Statistics of the New Jersey Department of Health (see Table 18.1).

Scores for the same social variables were extracted from the data set for states and subjected to an identical analysis, and these results are also presented in Table 18.1.

It can be seen that, although three factors were extracted for both counties and states, the composition of the factors was quite different. For the states, Factor I appears to tap death rates and social integration (a low divorce rate and high residential stability), Factor II poverty, and Factor III urbanization. For the counties, the three factors appear to tap urban/social integration (Factor I), poverty/death rates (Factor II), and poverty/birth rate/migration (Factor III). Not only are the factors different, but those for the counties do not appear to be as easily interpretable.

For the states, scores on Factor I (death rates/social integration) were associated with suicide rates, while scores on Factors II (poverty) and III (urbanization) were associated with homicide rates. In contrast, none of the factor scores for counties were associated with suicide rates, while scores on Factors I (urban/social integration) and II (poverty/death rates) were associated with homicide rates.

Looking at the associations between the social variables and rates of personal violence, divorce rates were associated in the same direction (positively) with suicide rates for both counties and states, while poverty, urbanization, and population were associated in the same direction (positively) with homicide rates.

Table 18.1 A comparison of American states and New Jersey counties

States (n=48)

	FACTOR I	FACTOR II	FACTOR III	Pearson Correlations Suicide	Pearson Correlations Homicide
birth rate	-0.75#	-0.18	-0.16	0.34*	-0.01
death rate	0.78#	-0.28	0.05	-0.45*	-0.01
divorce rate	-0.69#	-0.07	0.12	0.78*	0.40*
median family income	-0.04	0.92#	0.27	-0.08	-0.20
% in poverty	0.05	-0.92#	0.04	-0.02	0.51*
% urban	-0.08	0.56#	0.73#	0.08	0.29*
population density	0.66#	0.50#	0.25	-0.50*	-0.08
females/males	0.87#	-0.15	0.29	-0.64*	0.19
population	0.17	0.02	0.88#	-0.19	0.42*
no house move	0.91#	-0.11	-0.05	-0.79*	-0.08
suicide rate	-0.76*	-0.06	0.04		
homicide rate	-0.14	-0.44*	0.66*		

Counties (n=21)

	FACTOR I	FACTOR II	FACTOR III	Pearson Correlations Suicide	Pearson Correlations Homicide
birth rate	-0.05	0.22	0.88#	-0.02	0.36
death rate	-0.03	0.92#	-0.05	-0.26	0.37*
divorce rate	-0.81#	-0.12	0.16	0.39*	-0.50*
median family income	0.05	-0.78#	-0.58#	0.12	-0.50*
% in poverty	0.41	0.66#	0.53#	0.01	0.84*
% urban	0.83#	0.20	-0.18	-0.23	0.54*
population density	0.84#	0.13	0.23	-0.33	0.67*
females/males	0.44	0.84#	-0.03	-0.03	0.75*
population	0.90#	-0.06	-0.21	-0.25	0.54*
no house move	0.38	0.17	-0.66#	0.22	0.13
suicide rate	-0.27	-0.03	-0.11		
homicide rate	0.66*	0.49*	0.33		

high loading (> 0.50)
* significant at the 5% level or better

Discussion

Although some of the simple correlations between individual social variables and rates of personal violence were similar, the results of the factor analysis were quite different. This emphasizes the importance of the choice of regions in determining the results. It would be of interest to extend the present study to one of all counties in the USA rather than using only those in one state in order to see if the larger sample might reveal a pattern of associations more similar to those obtained for the states of America.

Part Four: Application to Other Problems

Chapter 19

DIVORCE

Yeh and Lester (1987) explored the relationship between the rate with which married women participated in the labor market in the states of America and the divorce rates. They found that states where a higher proportion of married worked full-time and a lower proportion worked part-time had the higher divorce rates.

One problem with these single-variable studies is that one of many possible social indicators is studied for its relationship with some target variable, ignoring all of the other social indicators that might also correlate with the target variable.

The present study sought to apply the data set and methodology developed in Chapter 2 to identify clusters of related social variables for the states of America and to see which of these clusters were associated with the statewide divorce rates.

Results

The results of the factor analysis (a Principal Components extraction with a varimax rotation using SPSSX) are shown in Table 19.1.* Seven orthogonal (independent) factors were identified, which may be labelled on the basis of the variables loading most highly on them: I wealthy/urban, II elderly, III southern, IV socially stable, V unemployment, VI participation in the labor force, and VII dense/eastern.

The divorce rate was strongly correlated only with Factor IV (social stability), a factor with high loadings from the suicide rate, interstate migration, church attendance and alcohol consumption. The percentage of people currently divorced in the states was also correlated with this factor, but in addition with Factor VII (dense/eastern). There was a higher percentage of divorced people in the western states.

Interestingly, the percentage of separated people showed a different pattern of associations. The percentage of separated people was associated with Factors I (urban/wealthy), II (elderly), and III (southern). The

---

* The variables included for this factor analysis differ a little from those used in the factor analysis reported in Chapter 2.

percentage of separated people was higher in the more urban/wealthy states, the states with an older population and southern states.

Table 19.1 Results of the factor analysis of the social variables and the correlations between the factor scores and statewide divorce rates
(decimal points are omitted from factor loadings)

	Factor						
	I	II	III	IV	V	VI	VII
suicide rate	01	-23	01	-88#	-02	-02	-15
interstate migration	-02	-26	-04	-87#	-26	13	02
church attendance	-13	-25	-20	67#	-37	-22	31
alcohol consumption	35	16	-22	-57#	-13	35	23
population	62#	13	28	28	17	-18	-35
population density	53#	37	-02	37	05	07	50#
% urban population	92#	-08	14	-05	-05	-01	10
per capita income	81#	21	-21	-03	-09	40#	-18
median family income	76#	01	-24	08	06	52#	-12
% foreign born	86#	22	-05	-09	01	-16	15
crime rate	74#	01	18	-50#	09	08	12
gross state product	45#	-28	-06	-22	-29	30	-37
personal income	82#	23	-20	-09	-09	39	-17
% in poverty	-52#	-12	56#	05	04	-43#	07
latitude	02	05	-88#	08	12	26	-06
% black	-10	09	89#	25	15	07	10
homicide rate	20	-04	85#	-18	13	-23	-10
southerness	-25	-09	84#	-17	14	-13	-26
% Roman Catholic	61#	31	-41#	01	05	05	39
infant mortality	04	22	78#	31	17	-02	13
death rate	-12	75#	-03	32	-03	-48#	01
birth rate	-15	-93#	-04	-14	-16	-08	-10
% voting for Reagan	05	-61#	-24	-26	-44#	-10	-08
% elderly	-07	64#	-24	19	-22	-59#	-01
% young	-34	-91#	06	04	07	-05	04
median age	31	90#	-05	-01	-02	-21	01
	Factor						
	I	II	III	IV	V	VI	VII
longitude	11	-56#	-15	-47#	-07	-09	-45#
females/males	08	55#	29	51#	19	-28	37
% born in state	-43#	03	04	83#	13	-12	-01
females in labor force	16	01	-28	-11	-35	76#	10
males in labor force	22	-33	-35	-04	-31	75#	-04
employment ratio	07	-13	-29	-11	-50#	70#	-01
strict gun control	26	18	02	62#	16	10	-02
unemployment rate	01	03	07	11	96#	-16	01
male unemployment rate	06	04	-06	13	92#	-17	-09
female unemployment rate	-07	-01	26	07	89#	-12	15
% of variance	26.7%	21.8%	13.4%	8.1%	7.4%	4.8%	3.3%
Correlation with:							
divorce rate	0.03	-0.17	0.15	-0.79*	0.01	0.02	-0.15
% divorced	0.20	-0.08	0.05	-0.82*	0.16	0.08	-0.25*
% separated	0.26*	0.24*	0.71*	0.08	0.17	0.22	0.19

high loading (> 0.40)
* significant at the 5% level or better

Discussion

The present study has shown that a set of social variables that may be used to describe the states of America form seven clusters. Of these seven clusters, only one, that pertaining to social stability, was associated with the divorce rate. Divorce rates were higher in states with less social stability (defined by the variables of a higher suicide rate, a high rate of interstate migration, low church attendance and a high rate of alcohol consumption).

Interestingly, the pattern of associations for the percentage of separated people in the states was quite different from that for the percentage of divorced people. This suggests that marriages end differently in different states, and that a formal versus an informal ending of the marriage may have different social determinants. Further research is clearly indicated to address this important question.

Chapter 20

FEMALE PARTICIPATION IN THE LABOR FORCE

Since 1963 the participation in the labor force by women has steadily increased while the participation by men has decreased (Bureau of Labor Statistics, 1977), and this has been true for both whites and non-whites. The increased participation by women is also found for those married and not married and for those with children and without children.

Blau and Ferber (1985) have suggested that the decline in the participation by men is a result of increasing time spent in school and the earlier retirement of older men. The increasing participation of women in the labor force may be a result of the changing attitudes of women toward what constitutes a fulfilling life (with more and more women thinking that work and a career are important components of a fulfilling life) and of the increasing difficulty that American families have in purchasing on a single salary the material goods they need.

Women's participation in the labor force varies greatly by state, and this variation provides an opportunity to search for social correlates of women's labor force participation, correlates which may provide some suggestions for hypothesized reasons for the involvement of women in the labor force. The present paper reports the results of a study of women's labor force participation in the states of the USA in 1980 using the data set developed for Chapter 2.

Results

The social indicators were subjected to a factor analysis using SPSSX with a principal components extraction and a varimax rotation. Six independent (orthogonal) factors were extracted (see Table 20.1). The participation of both women and men in the labor force was significantly associated with four of the six factor scores.

Factor II appears to tap south-versus-north and was negatively associated with participation in the labor force. People participate more in the labor force in the southern states. Factor III appears to tap urban/wealth and was positively associated with participation in the labor force. People participate more in the labor force in the more urban and wealthy states. Factor V seems to tap unemployment, and people participate less in the labor force where unemployment is high. Factor VI is related to the age composition in the state, and people participate less in the labor force in states with more elderly people.

Table 20.1 Results of the factor analysis and correlations of the factor scores with female participation in the labor force
(the decimal points are omitted from the factor loadings)

	Factor						correlation with labor force participation	
	I	II	III	IV	V	VI	males	females
divorce rate	87#	13	-08	-01	21	05	0.09	0.09
interstate migration	81#	-09	-13	-38	13	26	0.25*	0.29*
median family income	04	-26	79#	01	-13	33	0.48*	0.61*
% black	-22	87#	-11	12	-27	13	-0.25*	-0.40*
church attendance	-75#	-15	-09	-27	27	-07	-0.02	0.05
% Roman Catholic	-02	-40	66#	01	-36	-12	0.22	0.19
birth rate	07	-04	-25	-15	75#	52	-0.02	0.28*
% voting for Reagan	20	-21	-02	-44	62#	25	0.17	0.39*
southernness	21	83#	-32	17	12	02	-0.43*	-0.43*
% urban	12	19	89#	-04	15	06	0.19	0.20
% separated	-04	70#	27	07	-50#	20	-0.05	-0.20
% divorced	93#	02	11	14	17	03	0.15	0.13
per capita income	16	-21	84#	-11	-18	09	0.46*	0.51*
% over 65 years	-23	-14	-04	-09	-09	-91#	-0.27*	-0.51*
% under 15 years	-11	04	-41	07	60#	60#	-0.16	0.13
unemployment rate	-04	09	-01	98#	-07	01	-0.46*	-0.44*
male unemployment rate	-04	-03	06	95#	-01	-05	-0.42*	-0.37*
female unemployment	-03	26	-10	87#	-14	10	-0.45*	-0.47*
population	-14	37	65#	27	15	-24	-0.16	-0.16
population density	-37	01	59#	03	-47	-08	0.08	0.01
north-south	-06	-89#	10	09	-10	08	0.41*	0.42*
east-west	51#	-12	02	-04	69#	18	0.11	0.26*
alcohol consumption	58#	-27	36	-25	-33	13	0.49*	0.40*
death rate	-32	05	-07	09	-32	-84#	-0.40*	-0.60*
native born	-82#	06	-34	24	-01	-13	-0.31*	-0.27*
foreign born	13	02	86#	01	-08	-21	0.08	-0.01
infant mortality rate	-29	78#	03	14	-33	02	-0.37*	-0.45*
suicide rate	87#	-02	-09	-07	25	09	0.08	0.14
homicide rate	26	88#	11	17	12	-08	-0.38*	-0.42*
% of variance explained	24.7%	19.9%	17.4%	9.2%	8.3%	5.1%		
correlation with labor force participation:								
females	0.15	-0.36*	0.24*	-0.41*	-0.20	0.34*		
males	0.09	-0.43*	0.27*	-0.37*	0.05	0.57*		

high loading (> 0.40)
* significant at the 5% level or better

Factors I (low social integration) and III (conservative/west) were not related to participation in the labor force.

Discussion

People appear to participate more in the labor force in states which are in the north, which are more urban and wealthy, where unemployment is low and where there are fewer elderly. What is most surprising about these results is that the ecological correlations of female participation in the labor force were almost identical with the correlates of male participation in the labor force. In fact the two rates of participation were strongly associated ($r = 0.83$). This result is in direct contrast to the time series data reported by Blau and Ferber (1977) which showed a negative association over time in recent years. Clearly, the regional correlates (and possibly the determinants) of female participation in the labor force are different from the time-series correlates and determinants.

The fact that regional correlates of female participation in the labor force are similar to those for male participation suggests that regional variations in participation are affected more by the general social and economic factors in the states which affect everyone alike. For example, women were less likely to participate in the labor force where unemployment rates were high (for men and for women). Thus, where jobs are scarce, both sexes participate less in the labor force. Similarly, the greater the proportion of elderly in a state, the less women (and men) participate in the labor force, probably because a greater proportion of the people in those states are retired.

In particular, the present study throws doubt upon the use of female labor force participation as a measure of role conflict in women or social integration (Miley and Micklin, 1972; Newman, et al., 1973; Stack, 1978), since female labor force participation by state has a similar pattern of associations as male labor force participation.

The present study has been correlational and so cause-and-effect conclusions are not possible. However, the results of this study suggest that it would be of interest to explore the reasons for labor force participation and non-participation in women and men *in different regions of the country*. The present results suggest that these reasons may differ considerably from region to region.

Chapter 21

ALCOHOL CONSUMPTION

It has long been recognized that alcohol use and abuse and acts of suicide and homicide are related. Many attempted suicides and completed suicides are found to be intoxicated at the time of their suicidal action (Shneidman and Farberow, 1961), as are many murderers and their victims (Wolfgang, 1958). Much research has investigated suicidal behavior in alcohol abusers, and several reviews of this research have appeared (e.g., Lester, 1983). For example, Zmuc (1968) found that 45 percent of male completed suicides and four percent of female completed suicides were chronic alcohol abusers in Yugoslavia. Some psychiatrists have viewed suicidal behavior and alcohol abuse as similar self-destructive behaviors, and Menninger (1938) called alcohol abuse *chronic suicide*.

In addition, sociological studies of the correlations between rates of suicide and rates of alcohol use and abuse, both over regions and over time, have appeared. For example, Rushing (1968) found that mortality from suicide and from cirrhosis of the liver were associated over 40 age-by-sex-by-racial groups. Lester (1980b) reported that suicide rates in the 48 continental states of America in 1972 were positively associated with the per capita consumption of beer, spirits and wine, while homicide rates were not.

The present study sought to extend the methodology described in Chapter 2 to the study of the relationship between alcohol consumption in the states of America and rates of suicide and homicide in 1980. Thus, the study both replicates the earlier report on 1972 and searches for broader cultural patterns to account for the state variation in rates of personal violence.

Method

Data on 20 social variables were put into the factor analysis along with the three measures of alcohol consumption. These 23 social variables were factor analyzed using SPSSX Factor with a PC extraction and a varimax rotation. Seven factors were identified, and the factor scores correlated with the rates of personal violence.

Results

The bivariate Pearson correlations between the social variables and the rates of suicide and homicide are shown in Table 21.1 along with the results of the factor analysis and the correlations between the factor scores and rates of suicide and homicide. It can be seen that the consumption of alcohol was positively associated with suicide rates but not with homicide rates.

Table 21.1 Results of the correlational analysis
(Factor loadings are shown without a decimal point)

	Pearson Correlation		Factors					
	Suicide Rate	Homicide Rate	I	II	III	IV	V	VI
divorce rate	0.78*	0.40*	-31	69#	45	-04	-05	04
interstate migration	0.80*	0.02	-07	71#	55#	-12	21	06
% black	-0.30	0.68*	-78#	-20	-36	07	-06	26
church attendance	-0.49*	-0.26*	21	-67#	-03	-06	52#	-17
% Roman Catholic	-0.10	-0.23	58#	28	-41	48	04	-19
% voting Republican	0.35*	-0.18	13	05	78#	01	42	-05
% married women								
working full-time	0.15	0.42*	-61#	25	-05	-24	36	53#
working part-time	-0.17	-0.82*	93#	-01	-05	09	22	15
% urban	0.08	0.29*	01	12	07	95#	11	01
birth rate	0.34*	-0.01	-02	-19	87#	-10	12	18
unemployment rate	-0.11	0.23	-07	-15	-16	07	-85#	-04
% over 65	-0.33*	-0.18	11	-12	-37	-12	15	-76#
females in labor force	0.08	-0.38*	40	30	-05	08	45	64#
east-west	0.60*	0.06	05	23	85#	08	-11	06
north-south	-0.09	-0.80*	91#	04	01	-16	-13	14
median family income	-0.08	-0.20	45	14	-05	68#	-03	37
population	-0.19	0.42*	-17	-13	-18	65#	-28	-06
population density	-0.50	-0.08	19	-12	-61#	54#	14	-07
Southernness	0.20	0.77*	-91#	-03	14	-08	-23	06
crime rate	0.43*	0.36*	-08	52#	10	72#	-10	11
consumption of:								
beer	0.42*	-0.17	38	66#	16	10	21	04
wine	0.34*	-0.03	33	74#	-15	44	-02	07
spirits	0.36*	-0.01	19	82#	-18	08	22	15
percent of variance			25.2%	20.5%	15.6%	8.6%	7.2%	5.4%
Pearson correlation:								
suicide rate			-0.12	0.67*	0.55*	-0.04	-0.09	-0.03
homicide rate			-0.85*	0.13	0.01	0.32*	-0.15	-0.04

The factor analysis produced six factors which are shown in Table 21.1. The factors may be labelled crudely by means of the social indicators with the highest loadings. Factor I appears to reflect a north-south variation, Factor II alcohol consumption/social integration, Factor III an east-west variation, Factor IV urban environment, Factor V unemployment, and Factor VI youthfulness.

Alcohol consumption loaded on the factor reflecting social integration (the divorce rate, interstate migration, and church attendance). Scores on this factor were correlated with suicide rates. Where social integration was less and alcohol consumption higher, suicide rates were higher. Suicide rates also showed an east-west variation while homicide rates correlated with the urban factor and showed a north-south variation.

Discussion

The present study confirmed the earlier study by Lester (1980b) in that alcohol consumption in the states of America was positively associated with the suicide rate (but not with the homicide rate). However, the present analysis showed that alcohol consumption was higher in states with less social integration. The present study has focused on *alcohol consumption;* future studies could focus on alcohol abuse as well.

The search for broad cultural patterns, therefore, was successful. There are states in the USA where people are more likely to be residentially newcomers and divorced, less likely to be attached to churches, and also drink more beer, wine and spirits, and who have higher rates of suicide. These indices of social disorganization are highly inter-correlated, and it is not possible on the basis of these regional studies to assign one of the variables a primary causal role.

Interestingly, this sociocultural study has produced results that are congruent with studies on individuals. Just as psychiatric studies have shown that suicidal behavior is especially common in those who abuse alcohol and that suicidal individuals frequently are intoxicated at the time of their suicidal act, the present study has shown that regions where alcohol is consumed more also have have higher suicide rates.

Chapter 22

UNEMPLOYMENT

There has been some scholarly interest in the economic correlates of unemployment rates in different regions. For example, Lingle and Jones (1978) searched for economic correlates of the female unemployment rate in large Standard Statistical Metropolitan Areas and identified the median annual income of women working full time and the percentage of the female labor force married and living with a spouse as significant correlates.

The present chapter explores whether the social and economic variables from the data set used in Chapter 2 are associated with male and female unemployment rates.

Method

Thirty one of the variables from the data set described in Chapter 2 were subjected to a factor analysis using SPSSX, with a principal components extraction and a varimax rotation.

Results And Discussion

Male unemployment rates were most strongly associated with interstate migration and female participation in the labor force (see Table 22.1). Female unemployment rates were most strongly associated with male and female participation in the labor force, the vote for Reagan as President, and the percentage of blacks. There were differences in the correlates of male and of female unemployment rates. (Male and female unemployment rates were, however, strongly associated: Pearson r = 0.77).

Six orthogonal (independent) factors were identified (see Table 22.1). Looking at the variables most highly loaded on the factors, the factors appeared to tap: wealth (I), social instability (II), "southerness" (III), birth rate (IV), age (V), and population size (VI).

The factor scores for these six factors were correlated with the male and female unemployment rates (see Table 22.1). The pattern of associations were different for males and females. Male unemployment was associated with scores on Factor VI (population size) while female unemployment rates were associated with scores on Factor III (southern).

Interestingly, the social and economic variables in the present data set seemed to be only weakly associated with unemployment rates. In contrast, participation in the labor force was moderately associated with several factor scores (see Chapter 20). It may be that different socioeconomic variables would correlate more strongly with unemployment rates, and future research may be more successful in identifying these variables.

Table 22.1 Results of the factor analysis of the social indicators and the correlations of factor scores with unemployment rates

	Factor						Correlation with unemployment rates	
	I	II	III	IV	V	VI	male	female
divorce	-05	88#	10	17	02	-01	-0.06	0.02
interstate migration	-08	84#	-10	28	19	28	-0.40*	-0.29*
church attendance	-06	-71#	-19	36	-18	33	-0.19	-0.23
alcohol consumption	36	55#	-19	-20	30	38	-0.20	-0.29*
suicide rate	-06	89#	-04	23	01	-01	-0.10	-0.12
% born in state	-37	-82#	06	-07	-15	-20	0.25*	0.21
% black	-15	-21	91#	-16	04	-02	0.08	0.42*
southernness	-33	24	78#	08	-14	-29	0.12	0.31*
% separated	21	-07	80#	-33	20	09	0.06	0.29*
% divorced	12	92#	01	05	06	-19	0.07	0.07
% immigrants	87#	11	04	-15	-19	10	0.03	-0.03
% Roman Catholic	68#	-07	-30	-31	01	33	0.09	-0.09
% urban	88#	11	20	16	04	05	0.01	-0.05
% in poverty	-55#	-07	53#	14	-43	01	0.04	0.27*
gross state product	45#	31	-09	32	36	-18	-0.30*	-0.38*
personal income	85#	17	-18	-21	35	-10	-0.07	-0.25*
median family income	76#	-02	-18	-06	54#	-14	0.07	-0.14
per capita income	84#	11	-18	-18	37	-11	-0.06	-0.25*
population	61#	-16	31	-09	-20	-50#	0.26*	0.15
population density	59#	-40	10	-35	01	40	0.09	0.13
% elderly	03	-21	-30	-41	-72#	11	-0.01	-0.14
% children	-42	-07	08	82#	15	-05	-0.01	0.13
females in labor force	18	12	-32	-07	72#	21	-0.42*	-0.45*
males in labor force	23	06	-38	25	79#	07	-0.37*	-0.47*
latitude	07	-10	-83#	-14	27	-05	0.10	-0.16
longitude	02	55#	-20	59#	02	-32	-0.09	-0.18
death rate	-01	-32	-05	-60#	-64#	03	0.15	0.08
birth rate	-23	12	-06	92#	13	-06	-0.21	-0.14
% vote for Reagan	02	26	-28	73#	05	19	-0.36*	-0.46*
infant mortality rate	01	-29	82#	-23	-06	04	0.17	0.39*
homicide rate	12	28	85#	07	-25	-17	0.14	0.33*
percent of variance	27%	22%	16%	9%	6%	4%		
Correlation with:								
male unemployment	0.02	-0.11	0.08	-0.21	-0.18	-0.39*		
female unemployment	-0.14	-0.08	0.39*	-0.18	-0.13	-0.21		

loading greater than 0.45
* significant at the 5% level or better

Chapter 23

THE DEATH PENALTY

Yang and Lester (1989a) found that continental states in 1960 with no death penalty were characterized by larger populations, were less southern, and had lower violent crime rates. The present chapter sought to examine social correlates of the presence of a death penalty in a state in 1980 by applying a factor analytic technique to a different and broader set of social characteristics than that used in the Yang and Lester (1989a) study using the factors extracted from the data set described in Chapter 2.

Thirty eight states had the death penalty for all or part of 1980 while ten did not have a death penalty. The presence of a death penalty was associated with the crime rate, male unemployment, the percentage born in-state, the percentage of young and elderly, the percentage separated, latitude and "southerness", the percentage of blacks, and the divorce rate (see Table 23.1).

Table 23.1 Correlations between the social variables and the presence of a death penalty

	Point biserial r		Point biserial r
divorce rate	0.25*	latitude	-0.33*
interstate migration	0.32*	longitude	0.17
median family income	-0.08	alcohol consumption	0.11
% black	0.29*	death rate	-0.21
church attendance	-0.24	% under 15 years	0.10
% Roman Catholic	-0.15	% born in state	-0.36*
birth rate	0.14	% immigrants	0.13
% voting for Reagan	0.07	infant mortality rate	0.22
southern index	0.32*	median age	-0.06
% urban	0.17	% in poverty	0.23
% separated	0.41*	gross state product	0.09
% divorced	0.20	personal income	0.03
per capita income	-0.04	unemployment rate	-0.17
% over 65 years	-0.27*	male unemployment	-0.26*
females in labor force	0.01	female unemployment	0.01
males in labor force	0.01	employment ratio	0.06
gun control strictness	-0.06	crime rate	0.25*
population	0.09	females/males	-0.02
population density	-0.02		

* significant at the 5% level or better

Looking at factor scores, the presence of a death penalty was associated with scores on Factors II and IV (see Table 23.2). States with less social integration (divorce, interstate migration and low church attendance) and those in the south were more likely to have a death penalty.

Table 23.2 Correlations between the factor scores and the presence of a death penalty

Factor I	urban/wealth	0.10
Factor II	social disintegration	0.27*
Factor III	age	-0.14
Factor IV	southern	0.43*
Factor V	labor force participation	-0.03
Factor VI	unemployment	-0.17
Factor VII	Roman Catholicism	0.08

* significant at the 5% level or better

The results of both the present study and the earlier study by Yang and Lester indicate that the death penalty is more likely to be found in southern states. Some of the variables used in the study of 1960 (such as the ingenuousness of legislatures) were not available for 1980, and so some of the findings for 1960 cannot be cross-validated in 1980. However, the present study identifies social correlates of the presence of a death penalty in the states of America that can be replicated in future research.

Part Five: Conclusions

Chapter 24

EPISTEMOLOGICAL CONSIDERATIONS

The studies reported in this book make an important contribution to the understanding of the social correlates (and possible the social causes) of suicide and homicide rates in America. The studies also serve to confirm various hypotheses about suicide and homicide, such as those proposed by Durkheim (1897) for suicide and by Gastil (1971) for homicide. However, these issues have been discussed at the appropriate places throughout the book. This chapter will consider, instead, some epistemological implications of the research.

Recently, two critiques of the sociological approach to the study of suicide have appeared (Taylor, 1989; Moksony, 1989) which are remarkably congruent. They both suggest that sociologists have failed to demonstrate the influence of the *society* on suicide. The present chapter will review the arguments made by Taylor and Moksony in support of this proposition and then explore whether any research does meet their criteria.

Steve Taylor

Taylor (1990) described one major tradition in the sociological study of suicide as scientific and grounded in positivism, in which suicidal behavior is explained in terms of various social variables. Durkheim (1897) was the first sociologist to propose a systematic theory of suicide, and he made a clear distinction between explaining individual cases of suicide and explaining the society's suicide rate. Societal suicide rates were stable and could be explained sociologically.

In his book on suicide, Durkheim demonstrated associations between social variables (such as religious affiliation and marriage) and societal suicide rates. According to Taylor, Durkheim did not, however, mean to suggest that religious affiliation or marriage in themselves caused the differences in suicide rates. Rather, Durkheim used these associations to reveal a common underlying cause of suicide, which was the extent to which people are integrated and regulated by the society. Durkheim was searching for underlying and unobservable mechanisms and causal processes.

Later sociologists have forsaken the task of searching for invisible but real corrective forces acting upon individuals in a society and pursued instead a more empirical study of the relationships between observable social phenomena and suicide. They then view suicide as caused by these *external* social factors.

Ferenc Moksony

Moksony (1990) critiqued recent ecological studies of suicide, particular those of spatial differences in the suicide rate over the different areas of cities. The early studies of this by Cavan (1928) and Schmid (1928) attributed the spatial pattern of suicide in cities to their location in the ecological structure of the city. For example, those areas of the city with higher suicide rates tended to have an increased turnover in their population which Cavan saw as impeding the development of both a coherent system of norms and values governing behavior and stable social relationships.

Moksony argued that recent studies, such as Maris's (1969) or McCulloch and Philip's (1972) use aggregate data to describe relationships between various characteristics of the population in each area of the city to the suicide rate. These studies tend to explore the effects of the *composition* of the population in an area on the suicide rate rather than the area as an *environment*. For example, if areas have high numbers of migrants, then the suicide rate is predicted to be high because migrants have higher suicide rates. Cavan and Schmid, according to Moksony, would instead have treated the high proportion of migrants as a characteristic of the area and sought to show that this characteristic of the area impeded the development of a stable social life for everyone in the area, newcomers and old timers alike.

Moksony felt that his characterization of modern ecological studies was correct because the investigators often cast their studies as a preliminary step leading to a study in which the individuals would be directly observed. For example, if areas with many socially deviant individuals have higher suicide rates, the next step is usually to study suicidal behavior in the socially deviant and non-deviant people without regard to where they live (McCulloch and Philip, 1972).

An Examination Of Research

Both Taylor and Moksony have made the point, then, that sociologists have not studied the effect of society *qua* society on suicide rates. Rather, sociologists have studied the impact of social variables as causal agents in themselves on the suicide rate of individuals in the society. Is there any research which might satisfy Taylor and Moksony?

Immigrants

There is research on immigrants which has shown that the suicide rate of immigrant groups from different nations to the USA (Sainsbury and Barraclough, 1968) and to Australia (Lester, 1972) are in the same rank order as the suicide rates from their home nations.

This means that these individuals have been shaped by their home nations in the years before they emigrated so that the pattern of suicidal involvement characteristic of their nation is carried with them to their new home.

The problem with these studies is that the immigrants also brought with them a particular gene pool and physiological state. Thus, their suicide rate in their new nation may be proportional to the suicide rate in their home nation because of the similarity in genetic structure or brain chemistry.

In contrast to these studies which perhaps suggest the influence of the society of birth, Burvill, et al. (1983) showed that Irish, Scottish and English immigrants to Australia changed the methods that they used for suicide toward the Australian pattern. For the Irish immigrants this meant using active methods for suicide less often, while for the Scots and English immigrants it meant using active methods more often. This research seems to suggest the influence of the current society on the immigrants suicidal behavior.

Factor Analysis

In the present volume, we have analyzed the association between social variables and the suicide rate by subjecting them to a factor analysis in order to identify factors, or clusters, of related variables. The factor scores were then correlated with the suicide rates. We found, for example, that a cluster of variables including divorce rates, rates of interstate migration, and church attendance correlated most strongly with the suicide rates of the states of the USA. This research, because of the use of factor analysis rather than multiple regression, does not imply that any of these three variables is more important than the other two in this association. It also does not imply that these three social variables cause the state suicide rates. Rather the study implies that there is a larger social characteristic, manifested perhaps in the states' divorce rates, migrant composition and religious patterns, which is associated with suicide rates. This higher order characteristic, whatever it may be called (though low social integration seems a good possibility) seems close to satisfying Taylor's and Moksony's requirement for a *societal* or *areal* effect.

More detailed analyses in this book have shown that the higher order characteristic (perhaps indicating low social integration) is associated with the suicide rate of males and females, whites and blacks, and those of all ages. Thus, the association has generality and, in particular, despite the fact that one of the variables loading on the factor is the divorce rate, unpublished analyses have shown that the association is found for those of each marital status.

A study by Yang and Lester (1989c) also seems to satisfy some of the requirements of Taylor and Moksony. Yang and Lester explored the relationship between married women working (part-time and full-time) in the states of America with the suicide and homicide rates of the states. They found that, in states where married women were more likely to work full-time, the suicide rates of married men and married women were higher, but not the suicide rates of single, divorced or widowed men and women. However, the more often married women worked full-time, the higher the homicide rates in men and women of each marital status. This latter association seems to satisfy the demonstration of areal effect in which the behavior of one group (married women working) seems to be an index of some more fundamental or basic characteristic of the areas which affects the behavior of everyone.

Societal System Principles

Angyal (1941, 1965), a personality theorist, argued for a holistic position both for the consideration of the individual mind and for the society in which the individual lives. For the person, he discussed possibilities for the *system principle*, the pattern that organizes all of the component process of the person's mind. Similarly, for the society, he argued that the individual valences and demand qualities present in the society that impact upon the individual are organized into axiomatic values, which are themselves organized into systems of axioms. These systems of axioms then form a system principle for the society. Although he gave no examples of possible societal system principles, the distinction between democracy and totalitarianism can be seen as referring to a societal system principle, as might a conservative versus a liberal government.

In his analysis of societies, Parsons (1966) distinguished between primitive, archaic, advanced intermediate, and modern societies. These distinctions are really definitions of the system principles of different types of society as they developed over the centuries (Lester, 1984).

If we could classify a sample of modern societies according to such high level system principles and then compare the suicide rates of the nations in classification, again we would have come close to satisfying the requirements of Taylor and Moksony of demonstrating a possible societal effect on suicide rates.

Discussion

There is the suspicion that the issue raised by Taylor and Moksony may be a special case of the holistic/atomistic debate. Holistic theorists like to view the system (be it an individual mind or a society) as a whole, and they dislike analyzing the parts. However, a holistic analysis raises the question of the cause of the association. If we found, for example, that some broad characteristic of societies was associated with the suicide rate of those societies, then we would likely wonder how this association came about. The answer to such a question typically demands a non-holistic approach. From social integration, for example, we tend to move toward an examination of the various social customs that might affect social integration, and we eventually move to an examination of the impact of these customs on the individual. Then we will have laid ourselves open to the Taylor and Moksony criticisms.

For example, if we consider Eastern and Western European nations, which differ in democratic versus communist governments, it is hard not to consider specific differences in some features of the society, such as the freedom of the press, and difficult not to consider the impact of these characteristics on specific subgroups, such as the young and the old.

However, even if research and theorizing often moves toward an atomistic analysis, it would be intellectually satisfying if we could first demonstrate a societal or areal effect.

Chapter 25

CONCLUSIONS

This book has introduced a number of new approaches to the study of suicide and homicide and described some important results, and they will be reviewed briefly in this concluding chapter.

Factor Analysis

First, this book has made a strong argument for the use of factor-analytic techniques of data analysis rather than multiple regression. Multiple regression is a tool used extensively by economists who are concerned with using the past economic performance of a nation to predict future performance. Although a theoretical understanding of the factors which affect the economy should prove useful in choosing the predictor variables, multiple regression does not necessarily provide direct confirmation of the underlying theory.

In contrast, factor analysis is less concerned with prediction, but rather with identifying basic clusters of the variables chosen for analysis. In studies of the regional variation of suicide and homicide rates, where no one is seriously interested in predicting the suicide rate or the homicide rate of a particular state in, say, 1980 (after all, we know what it was), factor analysis makes much more sense than multiple regression.

Statistics, surprisingly, has been subject to fashion and fads. Factor-analysis was once very popular, but in recent years has been replaced by multiple regression in popularity. There are also differences by discipline. Economists often are puzzled when factor-analyses are presented to them; psychologists, who are often interested in identifying clusters of related items on psychological inventories, are familiar with factor-analytic techniques. Perhaps as someone trained in psychology, who subsequently became interested in the sociological study of suicide, I am willing to explore the use of factor-analytic techniques for the regional study of personal violence, as I have done in this book.

The reaction of readers of this volume will prove to be one test of the usefulness of this statistical approach. If you find the results of interest, provocative of further research, and of relevance to theory, then I will have proven my case.

Suicide And Homicide

By coming to the sociological study of suicide after my formal academic education, I have never viewed Durkheim as the major sociological theorist in the *contemporary* study of suicide. I am aware, of course, that sociologists almost always seek to base their research on his ideas. However, I read the three major sociological theories on suicide, those of Durkheim, Henry and Short, and Gibbs and Martin, at the same time, and I concluded that Henry and Short's theory was, for me, the most useful.

As a result, I have always seen suicide and homicide as both worthy of study simultaneously, for that is what Henry and Short argued in their book. Most sociologists, following Durkheim, ignore homicide.

The inclusion of homicide in this volume is made therefore, partly because it is an ideal behavior with which to compare suicide. Is an individual's anger directed inwards (resulting in suicide) or outwards (resulting in homicide)? Do nations aggress inwardly or outwardly? However, homicide is an important behavior, worthy of study in its own right, and its inclusion here need no justification other than that.

Elsewhere (Lester, 1987b), I have reviewed the evidence that suicide and homicide may be opposed behaviors, showing opposite relationships with social variables in regional studies of personal violence. The evidence presented in this book is not supportive of this position. The factor scores for the clusters of social variables used in the present set of analyses do *not* correlate with suicide and homicide rates in opposite directions. It appears rather that homicide demands a very different theoretical explanation from that provided for suicide.

Durkheim's Theory

The factor analysis of the social variables for the states of the USA identified a cluster of variables which included divorce, inter-state migration, church attendance, and alcohol consumption. This factor was named in this book "social disintegration", and certainly it does appear to tap Durkheim's concept.

Interestingly, no factor was identified which appeared to tap Durkheim's concept of social regulation. This may, of course, be simply a result of the variables included in the data set. However, the states of the USA may very well differ little in their degree of social regulation, and thus it would be difficult to measure any differences.

In some preliminary *international* studies of social variables (Lester, 1989c), I have been able to identify factors which may assess both social integration and social regulation, and this perhaps is a result of greater between-nation differences in the degree of social regulation.

The results of the present set of studies does support a modified version of Durkheim's theory of suicide. As Johnson (1965) has proposed, suicide is negatively associated with social integration: the less social integration of a region, the higher its suicide rate. (Durkheim himself proposed a U-shaped function relating social integration and suicide which has not been confirmed.)

A Subculture Of Violence

A major explanation for regional variations in homicide has been that there are regions with a subculture of violence. In the USA, the best indicator of this has been "southerness" (Gastil, 1971), and the present set of studies has indicated that the factor assessing "southerness" is strongly associated with homicide rates, overall and in specific subgroups of the population, males and females, young and old (except for the very oldest), for blacks and whites (though less strongly for blacks), and for most major methods of committing homicide.

Interestingly, homicide rates in the USA were higher in those states with lower levels of social integration, as were suicide rates, though less strongly, suggesting that a Durkheimian-based theory of homicide might have some usefulness if one were to be proposed.

Epistemological Considerations

In the previous chapter a distinction was made between identifying specific social characteristics that are associated with, and perhaps determine, the suicide rates of regions and identifying an abstract social quality that is associated with the suicide rates of regions. The present set of studies has show, for example, that the divorce rate of a region is a consistent correlate of the suicide rate, in almost all groups in the USA, and both within other countries and between other countries. Changes in the divorce rate are also associated with changes in the suicide rate. Thus, divorce was the most powerful associate of suicide rates in this set of studies.

However, scores on Factor II (social disintegration) were also consistently associated with regional suicide rates, and this was seen as support for Taylor's demand that sociologists demonstrate that a social quality with a high level of abstraction, social integration, rather than one possible facet of it, was associated with suicide rates.

Extensions

Finally, the set of studies was extended to include studies of other social characteristics as target variables. The set of social variables was found to provide some suggestions for regional correlates of such characteristics as unemployment, divorce, alcohol consumption and the death penalty.

References

Abe, K., Egashira, K., & Suzuki, T. Suicide seasonality and economic growth. *Stress Medicine*, 1986, 2, 79-81.

Angyal, A. *Foundations for a science of personality*. New York: Commonwealth Fund, 1941.

Angyal, A. *Neusosis and treatment*. New York: Wiley, 1965.

Anon. *Statistical Review of England and Wales, 1961*. London: HMSO, 1963.

Anon. *Complete Atlas of the British Isles*. London: Reader's Digest Association, 1965.

Anon. *US apparent consumption of alcoholic beverages based on state sales, taxation, or receipt data*. Rockville: National Institute on Alcohol Abuse & Alcoholism, 1985.

Blau, F. B., & Ferber, M. A. Women in the labor market. *Women and Work*, 1985, 1, 19-49.

Breault, K. D. Suicide in America. *American Journal of Sociology*, 1986, 92, 628-656.

Breault, K. D., & Barkley, K. A comparative analysis of Durkheim's theory of suicide. *Sociological Quarterly*, 1982, 23, 321-331.

Bureau of Labor Statistics. *U.S. Working Women*. Washington, DC: US Department of Labor, 1977.

Burvill, P., McCall, M., Woodings, T., & Stenhouse, N. Comparison of suicide rates and methods in English, Scots, and Irish immigrants in Australia. *Social Science & Medicine*, 1983, 17, 705-708.

Cavan, R. S. *Suicide*. Chicago: University of Chicago, 1928.

Clarke, R. V., & Lester, D. *Suicide: closing the exits*. New York: Springer Verlag, 1989.

Davis, P. *Suicidal adolescents*. Springfield: Thomas, 1983.

Department of Census and Statistics. *Census of population, 1971*. Colombo, Sri Lanka: Department of Census and Statistics, 1978.

Diggory, J. C., & Lester, D. Suicide rates of men and women. *Omega*, 1976, 7, 95-101.

Doan, T. A. *User's manual - RATS*. Evanston: Var Econometrics, 1988.

Durkheim, E. *Suicide*. Paris: Felix Alcan, 1897

Ellner, M. Research on international suicide. *International Journal of Social Psychiatry*, 1977, 23, 187-194.

Field, F. B. Mortality rates and aggression management indices. *Journal of Health & Human behavior*, 1963, 4, 70-78.

Gastil, R. Homicide and a regional culture of violence. *American Sociological Review*, 1971, 36, 412-427.

Henry, A. F., & Short, J. F. *Suicide and homicide*. New York: Free Press, 1954.

Humphrey, J. A., & Kupferer, H. J. Pockets of violence. *Diseases of the Nervous System*, 1977, 38, 833-837.

International Labor Office. *Yearbook of labor statistics, 1976*. Geneva: ILO, 1976.

Johnson, B. D. Durkheim's one cause of suicide. *American Sociological Review*, 1965, 30, 875-886.

Kearney, R. N., & Miller, B. D. Sex-differential patterns of internal migration in Sri Lanka. *Peasant Studies*, 1983, 10, 223-250.

Kearney, R. N., & Miller, B. D. The spiral of suicide and social change in Sri Lanka. *Journal of Asian Studies*, 1985, 45, 81-101.

Kowalski, G. S., Faupel, C. E., & Starr, P. D. Urbanism and suicide. *Social Forces*, 1987, 66, 85-101.

Langford, C. M. Fertility change in Sri Lanka since the war. *Population Studies*, 1981, 35, 285-306.

Lester, D. Suicide and homicide in open and closed societies. *Psychological Reports*, 1971, 29, 430.

Lester, D. Migration and suicide. *Medical Journal of Australia*, 1972, 1, 941-942.

Lester, D. A cross-national study of homicide and suicide. *Behavior Science Research*, 1974, 9, 307-318.

Lester, D. Variation of suicide and homicide by latitude and longitude. *Perceptual & Motor Skills*, 1980a, 51, 1346.

Lester, D. Alcohol and suicide and homicide. *Journal of Studies on Alcohol*, 1980b, 41, 1220-1223.

Lester, D. Freedom of the press and personal violence. *Journal of Social Psychology*, 1981, 114, 267-269.

Lester, D. *Why people kill themselves*. Springfield: Charles Thomas, 1983.

Lester, D. Systems theories of personality: some Parsonian implications. *Psychology*, 1984, 21(1), 12-14.

Lester, D. Regional variation in suicide and homicide. *Suicide & Life-Threatening Behavior*, 1985, 15, 110-116.

Lester, D. Southern subculture, personal violence (suicide and homicide), and firearms. *Omega*, 1986-1987, 17, 183-186.

Lester, D. Religion, suicide and homicide. *Social Psychiatry*, 1987a, 22, 99-101.

Lester, D. Suicide and homicide: are they polar opposites? *Behavioral Sciences & the Law*, 1987b, 5, 49-60.

Lester, D. An availability-acceptability theory of suicide. *Activitas Nervosa Superior*, 1987c, 29, 164-166.

Lester, D. Social deviancy and suicidal behavior. *Journal of Social Psychology*, 1987d, 127, 339-340.

Lester, D. A regional analysis of suicide and homicide rates in the USA. *Social Psychiatry & Psychiatric Epidemiology*, 1988a, 23, 202-205.

Lester, D. Youth suicide. *Adolescence*, 1988b, 23, 955-958.

Lester, D. *Why women kill themselves*. Springfield: Thomas, 1988c.

Lester, D. Demographic attributions related to black suicide. *Journal of Social Psychology*, 1988d, 128, 407-409.

Lester, D. A regional analysis of suicide: the USA vs Sri Lanka. *Social Psychiatry & Psychiatric Epidemiology*, 1989a, 24, 143-145.

Lester, D. The spatial autocorrelation of states' suicide and homicide rates. *Perceptual & Motor Skills*, 1989b, 68, 218.

Lester, D. *Suicide from a sociological perspective*. Springfield: Charles Thomas, 1989c.

Lester, D., & Moksony, F. Ecological correlates of suicide in the United State and Hungary. *Acta Psychiatrica Scandinavia*, 1989, 79, 498-499.

Lingle, R. C., & Jones, E. B. Women's increasing unemployment. *American Economic Review*, 1978, 68(2), 84 -89.

Lynn, R. *Personality and national character*. Elmsford, NY: Pergamon, 1971.

Maris, R. *Social forces in urban suicide*. Homewood, IL: Dorsey, 1969.

Maris, R. The adolescent suicide problem. *Suicide & Life-Threatening Behavior*, 1985, 15, 91-109.

McCulloch, J. W., & Philip, A. E. *Suicidal behavior*. Elmsford, NY: Pergamon, 1972.

Menninger, K. *Man against himself*. New York: Harcourt, Brace & World, 1938.

Miley, J., & Micklin, M. Structural change and the Durkheimian legacy. *American Journal of Sociology*, 1972, 78, 657-673.

Moksony, F. Ecological analysis of suicide. In D. Lester (Ed.) *Understanding suicide*. Philadelphia: Charles, 1990, 121-138.

National Center for Health Statistics. *Vital Statistics of the United States*, 1980. US Government Printing Office, Washington DC, 1985.

Newman, J., Whittemore, K., & Newman, H. Women in the labor force and suicide. *Social Problems*, 1973, 21, 220-230.

Odland, J. *Spatial autocorrelation*. Beverly Hills: Sage, 1988.

Palmer, S. Characteristics of suicide in 54 nonliterate societies. *Life-Threatening Behavior*, 1971, 1, 178-183.

Parsons, T. *Societies*. Englewood Cliffs, NJ: Prentice-Hall, 1966.

Pescosolido, B. A., & Mendelsohn, R. Social causation or social construction. *American Sociological Review*, 1986, 51, 80-101.

Phillips, D. P. Teenage and adult temporal fluctuations in suicide and auto fatalities. In H. S. Sudak, A. B. Ford, & N. B. Rushforth (Eds.) *Suicide in the young*. Boston: John Wright, 1984, 69-80.

Quinn, B., Anderson, H., Bradley, M., Goetting, P., & Shriver, P. *Churches and church membership in the US*, 1980. Atlanta: Glenmary Research Center. 1982.

Renshaw, V., Trott, E. A., & Friedenberg, H. L. Gross state product by industry, 1963-1986. *Survey of Current Business*, 1988, May, 30-46.

Rushing, W. A. Alcoholism and suicide rates by status set and occupation. *Quarterly Journal of Studies on Alcohol*, 1968, 29, 399-412.

Sainsbury, P., & Barraclough, B. M. Differences between suicide rates. *Nature*, 1968, 220, 1252.

Sainsbury, P., Jenkins, J., & Levey, A. The social correlates of suicide in Europe. In R. Farmer & S. Hirsch (Eds.) *The suicide syndrome*. London: Croom Helm, 1980, 38-53.

Schmid, C. F. *Suicide in Seattle*, 1914-1925. Seattle: University of Washington, 1928.

Shneidman, E. S., & Farberow, N. L. *The cry for help*. New York: McGraw-Hill, 1961.

Stack, S. Suicide. *Social Forces*, 1978, 57, 644-653.

Stack, S. The effects of interstate migration on suicide. *International Journal of Social Psychiatry*, 1980a, 26, 17-25.

Stack, S. The effects of marital dissolution on suicide. *Journal of Marriage & the Family*, 1980b, 42, 83-91.

Stack, S. Religion and suicide. *Social Psychiatry*, 1980c, 15, 65-70.

Stack, S. Domestic integration and the rate of suicide. *Journal of Comparative Family Studies*, 1980d, 11, 249-260.

Stack, S. The effects of age composition on suicide in traditional and industrial socieities. *Journal of Social Psychology*, 1980e, 111, 143-144.

Stack, S. Comparative analysis of immigration and suicide. *Psychological Reports*, 1981a, 49, 509-510.

Stack, S. Divorce and suicide. *Journal of Family Issues*, 1981b, 2, 77-90.

Summers, R., & Heston, A. Improved international comparisons of real produce and its compopsition. *Review of Income & Wealth*, 1984, 30, 207-262.

Taylor, S. *Suicide, Durkheim and sociology*. In D. Lester (Ed.) *Understanding suicide*. Philadelphia: Charles, 1990, 225-236.

United Nations. *Demographic Yearbook*, 1982. New York: United Nations, 1984.

Whitt, H. P. The lethal aggression ratio and the suicide-murder ratio. *Dissertation Abstract*, 1969, 29B, 2624-2625.

Whitt, H. P. Comments on Stack's paper "Suicide: a decade review of the sociological literature." *Deviant Behavior*, 1985, 6, 229-231.

Whitt, H. P., Gordon, C. C., & Hofley, J. R. Religion, econmomic development and lethal aggression. *American Sociological Review*, 1972, 37, 193-201.

Wolfgang, M. E. *Patterns of homicide*. Philadelphia: University of Pennsylvania Press, 1958.

World Bank. *World Tables*. Baltimore: Johns Hopkins University Press, 1984.

Yang, B., & Lester, D. Which states have a death penalty? *Psychological Reports*, 1989a, 64, 1180.

Yang, B., & Lester, D. Which states have a death penalty: data from 1980. *Psychological Reports*, 1989b, 65, 185-186.

Yang, B., & Lester, D. The association between working women and personal violence (suicide and homicide) in married men and women. Pennsylvania Economic Association, Millersville, PA., 1989c.

Yeh, B. Y., & Lester, D. Statewide divorce rates and wives' participation in the labor market. *Journal of Divorce*, 1987, 11, 107-114.

Zmuc, M. Alcohol and suicide. *Alcoholism*, 1968, 4, 38-44.

Subject Index